DATE DUE

10-17-2011	

LINCOLN AND THE COMING
OF THE CIVIL WAR

Problems in American Civilization

UNDER THE EDITORIAL DIRECTION OF
George Rogers Taylor

LINCOLN AND THE COMING OF THE CIVIL WAR

EDITED WITH AN INTRODUCTION BY

Norton Garfinkle

Problems in American Civilization

READINGS SELECTED BY
THE DEPARTMENT OF AMERICAN STUDIES
AMHERST COLLEGE

D. C. HEATH AND COMPANY: Boston

INTRODUCTION

THE Civil War was the great crisis of American history. The need to resolve the contradiction between the equalitarian principles of the Declaration of Independence and the inferior status accorded Negroes posed the sharpest moral question Americans have ever faced. Concurrently, the effort to reconcile the federalist principles of the Constitution with the expanded power of the national government provided Americans with their most difficult political decision.

Lincoln guided the nation to a resolution of these problems. He charted a course and persuaded the people of the North to follow his leadership. Nathaniel Stephenson has remarked, "The history of the North" during this period is largely "the history of Lincoln himself."[1]

The eyes of Americans in 1858 were focused on the State of Illinois where Stephen A. Douglas, the leader of the Northern wing of the Democratic Party, was standing for re-election to the Senate. To deal with the burning political issue of slavery in the territories, Douglas urged the principle of "popular sovereignty," that the white inhabitants of each territory should decide for themselves the fate of slavery within their own borders. He maintained that this compromise solution to the territorial question would provide a practical basis for resolving the issues dividing the Northern and Southern states.

Opposed to Douglas in the race for the Senate was Abraham Lincoln. He urged that the problems of the day called for a general consideration of moral issues rather than a specific consideration of political policies. In the great debates of 1858, Lincoln took much the same position on policy questions as Douglas. He opposed Negro citizenship, supported the fugitive slave law, and repudiated the idea of interfering with slavery where it existed in the Southern States. But on the general question of the morality of slavery, Lincoln spoke boldly. He maintained that the two parties represented fundamentally opposed moral positions — that the Democratic Party represented those who considered slavery "right" while the Republican Party represented those who considered slavery "wrong."

Although Lincoln lost the Senate race, his stand on slavery captured the imagination of a significant segment of the voters in Illinois and other Northern States. It rallied the disparate elements of the Republican Party in opposition to compromise solutions of the territorial question and provided a solid foundation for Lincoln's successful campaign for the presidency in 1860.

The consequences of Lincoln's election to the presidency were profound. When the news reached the lower South, secession proceedings were initiated in seven

[1] Nathaniel W. Stephenson, *Abraham Lincoln and the Union* (New Haven: Yale University Press, 1918), p. 126.

states. Overnight, the problem of slavery in the territories became inextricably intertwined with the issues of union or disunion and of war or peace.

For the Republican Party, the period following the election of 1860 was a time of crisis. The imminence of disunion awakened support within the party for a compromise solution to the crucial dispute over slavery in the territories. Some Republicans seemed disposed to listen to Douglas' argument that popular sovereignty or some other compromise solution would effectively bar slavery from the territories. Others denounced any retreat from the position taken in the Republican platform. As leader of his party and chief of the new administration, Lincoln assumed the responsibility of forging a policy to deal with the crisis.

Four possible courses of action were available to the president-elect.

One possibility was to lend his support to the efforts to work out a compromise on the territorial question. This course was urged by Northern leaders who believed an effective compromise on the territorial question would keep the Southern States in the union on a voluntary basis. They argued that such a compromise sacrificed nothing material as slavery could not be profitably extended into territories unsuited to cotton growing.

A second procedure would be to recognize Southern independence and let the Southern States "go in peace." This was urged upon Lincoln by Northern and Southern leaders who believed that the right of secession was morally justified by the Declaration of Independence and legally permissible under the federal system established by the Constitution. They argued that the principle of self government would be violated if the Southern States were forced to remain in the union.

A third plan involved the withdrawal of federal troops from the Southern States while at the same time refusing to recognize Southern independence. This was advocated by Northerners who felt that it would lead to a peaceful reconstruction of the union. They held that the Southern States would return to the union on their own initiative when they discovered the disadvantages of independence.

A fourth option involved maintaining federal troops in the Southern States as a symbol of federal authority. Northern leaders, who felt that the union must be preserved even at the risk of war, supported this position. They believed that in order to prevent anarchy in the affairs of the nation, the authority of the union had to be maintained.

Lincoln adopted this last course of action. He used his power and prestige as leader of his party and chief of the new administration to prevent any compromise on the territorial question and to outlaw the secession movement.

The effect of this policy was direct and immediate. The seven states of the lower South seceded from the union and demanded the withdrawal of federal troops from their territory. Lincoln refused; Southern troops fired on the federal garrison at Fort Sumter in South Carolina; and Lincoln ordered the army to undertake military proceedings to reestablish federal authority in the Southern States.

Americans have divided sharply in their evaluations of Lincoln's role in the events leading to the Civil War. The lines were clearly drawn on this issue as early as 1861. Critics who felt that there was a basis of adjustment between the North and South condemned Lincoln for provoking a "needless war." Advocates who felt that firm action against the South was necessary praised Lincoln for his bold leadership.

Modern writers also disagree about the wisdom of Lincoln's pre-war policies. Some contend that he failed to adopt a course of action which might well have made possible the peaceful abolition of slavery. Others maintain that Lincoln's policy secured the abolition of slavery at the least possible cost.

Did Lincoln use his powers wisely? Or did the Civil War President lead the nation in the wrong direction? These questions are considered in this volume. The issues raised in Lincoln's day are restated and the alternatives available to the Civil War President are considered. The reader must decide for himself whether, in the light of available information, Lincoln chose the best course of action.

To contemporary Americans, the study of Lincoln's role in the events leading to the Civil War has a particular significance. The specific questions which faced Americans in the mid-nineteenth century no longer exist. But many of the general issues of Lincoln's day are still with us. Persistent conflicts between segregationists and integrationists call for an evaluation of the relation of the equalitarian principles of the Declaration of Independence to our patterns of race relations. Continuing international controversies call for a consideration of the relation between the principles of self-government and self-determination and the goal of international peace and order. Recurrent ideological conflicts between nations call for a clear decision concerning the use of war as an instrument of national policy. The study of Lincoln's response to these issues can perhaps contribute to our understanding both of the limits and the possibilities of action in dealing with the problems facing us today.

More than this, the study of Lincoln's career can contribute to a realistic appraisal of the function of political leadership in a democratic society. Does an understanding of the choices open to Lincoln strengthen the conclusion that political leaders play a crucial role in shaping the course of events? Or does a recognition of the complexity of the problems which Lincoln faced lead us to question how much even a strong leader can accomplish? As the reader considers these matters, he may well keep in mind a conclusion which Lincoln drew from his own experience in public life. He said, "There are few things wholly evil or wholly good. Almost everything especially of government policy is an inseparable compound of the two, so that our best judgment of the preponderance between them is continually demanded."

[NOTE: The quotation on page xi is from Howard K. Beale, "What Historians Have Said About the Causes of the Civil War," *Theory and Practice in Historical Study* (New York: Social Science Research Council, 1946), pp. 76–77. Reprinted by permission.]

CONTENTS

The Clash of Issues

"Lincoln is still an enigma, subject to strong disagreement. . . . His claims to greatness after the War began seem little questioned today. . . . About his part in the coming of war, there is still controversy. Some see in Lincoln a statesman who perceived and gave popular voice to the fundamental issues of his day, a leader whose abilities brought the nation through crisis to preservation of the Union and elimination of slavery. Others, however, picture him in the antebellum years as a skillful politician whose cleverness turned every situation to his own and his party's advantage. . . . Did his "house divided" speech call to the nation's attention a fundamental truth and set in motion a series of events that ultimately resolved the conflict in favor of union and freedom instead of disunion and expansion of slavery over the whole nation? Or did the speech merely call Abraham Lincoln to public attention in such a way as to put him finally in the White House and make war inevitable? Did his debates with Douglas clarify a great public issue that Douglas was beclouding and thereby lead to saving the Union? Or did Lincoln in these debates merely win for himself the presidency at the expense of precipitating a bloody war that Douglas as president might have avoided without loss to the nation? Did Lincoln's refusal to sanction compromise in December, 1860, save the country from further conflict over slavery in new territories to be acquired and preserve the Union from ultimate disruption or subjection to the rule of slaveholders made powerful through expansion? Or did it merely precipitate a war that could otherwise have been avoided without destruction of the Union?"

Howard K. Beale

Richard B. Hofstadter: LINCOLN AND THE SLAVERY QUESTION

Richard Hofstadter is one of the most perceptive contemporary students of American political leadership. In his study of The American Political Tradition and the Men Who Made It, *Hofstadter called for a reappraisal of the major figures of our past. Hofstadter's chapter on Lincoln, a portion of which is reprinted here, examines Lincoln's influence in shaping public opinion on the slavery question and raises serious questions concerning his role in the events leading to the Civil War.*

IF historical epochs are judged by the opportunities they offer talented men to rise from the ranks to places of wealth, power, and prestige, the period during which Lincoln grew up was among the greatest in history, and among all places such opportunities were most available in the fresh territory north and west of the Ohio River — the Valley of Democracy.

Abraham Lincoln was nineteen years old when Andrew Jackson was elected President. Like most of the poor in his part of the country, Thomas Lincoln was a Jacksonian Democrat, and his son at first accepted his politics. But some time during his eighteenth or nineteenth year Abraham went through a political conversion, became a National Republican, and cast his first vote, in 1832, for Henry Clay.

The National Republican (later Whig) Party was the party of internal improvements, stable currency, and conservative banking; Lincoln lived in a country that needed all three. If the Democrats spoke more emphatically about the equality of man, the Whigs, even in the West, had the most imposing and affluent men. That an ambitious youth should look to the more solid citizens of his community for political guidance was natural and expedient; the men Lincoln most respected in the Indiana town of his boyhood were National Republicans, great admirers of Henry Clay; and as Dennis Hanks mournfully recalled, Lincoln himself "allways Loved Hen Clay's speaches." With one exception, John Hanks, who turned Republican in 1860, Abraham was the only member of the Lincoln or Hanks families who deserted the Democratic Party.

After a few years of stagnation Lincoln advanced with the utmost rapidity in his middle twenties. While many of the stories about the hardships of his youth celebrated in Lincoln legendry are true, it is noteworthy that success came to him suddenly and at a rather early age. At twenty-four he was utterly obscure. At twenty-eight he was the leader of his party in the Illinois House of Repre-

Reprinted from *The American Political Tradition and the Men Who Made It* by Richard Hofstadter, pp. 99–103, 107–117, by permission of Alfred A. Knopf, Inc. Copyright 1948 by Alfred A. Knopf, Inc.

sentatives, renowned as the winner of the fight to bring the state capital to Springfield, extremely popular in both Sangamon County and the capital itself, and partner of one of the ablest lawyers in the state. Of his first years in Springfield Herndon writes: "No man ever had an easier time of it in his early days than Lincoln. He had . . . influential and financial friends to help him; they almost fought each other for the privilege of assisting Lincoln. . . . Lincoln was a pet . . . in this city." And, adds Herndon, "he deserved it." Success of this sort eases and fattens smaller men; for more restless souls it is a form of poison.

Like his "influential and financial friends," Lincoln belonged to the party of rank and privilege; it exacted a price from him. In time he was to marry into the family circle of Ninian Edwards, of whom it was once observed that he was "naturally and constitutionally an aristocrat and . . . hated democracy . . . as the devil is said to hate holy water." Lincoln's connection with such a tribe could only spur his loyalty to the democratic ways in which he had been brought up; he never did "belong," and Mary Todd's attitude toward him as a social creature was always disdainful.

In a letter written in 1858, discussing the growth of the Republican Party, he observed: "Much of the plain old Democracy is with us, while nearly all the old exclusive silkstocking Whiggery is against us. I don't mean all the Old Whig party, but nearly all of the nice exclusive sort." Lincoln's keen sense of not belonging to the "nice exclusive sort" was a distinct political asset. Throughout his early career, no doubt, it enabled him to speak with sincerity for Jeffersonian principles while supporting Hamiltonian measures. For public and private reasons alike he was touchy about attempts to

link him with the aristocrats because of his Whig affiliations, and once complained bitterly at being incongruously "put down here as the candidate of pride, wealth, and aristocratic family distinction."

And yet it was true that the young Lincoln fell short of being an outspoken democrat. In the social climate of Illinois he ranked as a moderate conservative. Running for re-election to the legislature in 1836, he submitted to a newspaper a statement of his views which included the following: "I go for all sharing the privileges of the government who assist in bearing its burdens. Consequently I go for admitting all whites to the right of suffrage who pay taxes or bear arms (by no means excluding females)." Now, the Illinois Constitution of 1818 had already granted the suffrage to all white male inhabitants of twenty-one or over without further qualification, so that Lincoln's proposal actually involved a step backward.

Lincoln's democracy was not broad enough to transcend color lines, but on this score it had more latitude than the democracy professed by many of his neighbors and contemporaries. One of the extraordinary things about his strangely involved personality is the contrast between his circumspectness in practical politics wherever the Negro was concerned, and his penetration of the logic of the proslavery argument, which he answered with exceptional insight. His keen onslaughts against slavery, in fact, carry the conviction of a man of far greater moral force than the pre-presidential Lincoln ever revealed in action. After 1854, when he renewed his study of the slavery question, Lincoln was particularly acute in showing that the logic of the defenders of slavery was profoundly undemocratic, not only in reference to the Southern scene, but for human relations everywhere. The essence of his position was that the principle of exclusion has no inner check; that arbitrarily barring one minority from the exercise of its rights can be both a precedent and a moral sanction for barring another, and that it creates a frame of mind from which no one can expect justice or security. "I am not a Know-nothing," he wrote to Speed:

How could I be? How can anyone who abhors the oppression of Negroes be in favor of degrading classes of white people? Our progress in degeneracy appears to me to be pretty rapid. As a nation we began by declaring that "all men are created equal." We now practically read it "all men are created equal except negroes." When the Know-nothings get control, it will read "all men are created equal, except negroes and foreigners and Catholics." When it comes to this, I shall prefer emigrating to some country where they make no pretense of loving liberty, — to Russia, for instance, where despotism can be taken pure, and without the base alloy of hypocrisy.

In Lincoln's eyes the Declaration of Independence thus becomes once again what it had been to Jefferson — not merely a formal theory of rights, but an instrument of democracy. It was to Jefferson that Lincoln looked as the source of his political inspiration, Jefferson whom he described as "the most distinguished politician of our history." "The principles of Jefferson are the definitions and axioms of free society," he declared in 1859. "The Jefferson party," he wrote privately at about the same time, "was formed upon its supposed superior devotion to the rights of men, holding the rights of property to be secondary only, and greatly inferior." The Democratic Party, he charged, had abandoned Jeffersonian tradition by taking the position that one man's liberty was absolutely nothing when it conflicted with another man's property. "Republicans," he added, in an utterly characteristic sentence which ought to be well remembered, "are for both the man and the dollar, but in case of conflict the man before the dollar." There is self-portraiture in the remark: one sees the moral idealism of the man; it is there, unquestionably, but he hopes that the world will never force it to obtrude itself.

The Declaration of Independence was not only the primary article of Lincoln's creed; it provided his most formidable political ammunition. And yet in the end it was the Declaration that he could not make a consistent part of his living work. The Declaration was a revolutionary document, and this too Lincoln accepted. One of his early public statements declares:

Any people anywhere being inclined and having the power have the right to rise up and shake off the existing government, and form a new one that suits them better. This is a most valuable, a most sacred right — a right which we hope and believe is to liberate the world.

Having said so much, he did not stop:

Any portion of such people that can may revolutionize and make their own of so much territory as they inhabit. More than this, *a majority of any portion of such people may revolutionize, putting down a minority, intermingled with or near about them,* who may oppose this movement. Such a minority was precisely the case of the Tories of our own revolution. It is a quality of revolutions not to go by old lines or old laws; but to break up both, and make new ones.

The principle is reiterated with firmness in the First Inaugural Address.

So Lincoln, the revolutionary theorist. There was another Lincoln who had a lawyer-like feeling for the niceties of established rules and a nationalist's reverence for constitutional sanction. This Lincoln always publicly condemned the abolitionists who fought slavery by extra-constitutional means — and condemned also the mobs who deprived them of their right of free speech and free press. This Lincoln, even before he was thirty, warned the young men of Springfield that disrespect for legal observances might destroy free institutions in America, and urged them to let reverence for the laws "become the political religion of the nation." This Lincoln suppressed secession and refused to acknowledge that the right of revolution he had so boldly accepted belonged to the South. The same Lincoln, as we shall see, refused almost to the last minute even to suppress rebellion by revolutionary means. The contradiction is not peculiar to Lincoln; Anglo-Saxon history is full of it. . . .

A story about Abraham Lincoln's second trip to New Orleans when he was twenty-one holds an important place in the Lincoln legend. According to John Hanks, when Lincoln went with his companions to a slave market they saw a handsome mulatto girl being sold on the block, and "the iron entered his soul"; he swore that if he ever got a chance he would hit slavery "and hit it hard." The implication is clear: Lincoln was half abolitionist and the Emancipation Proclamation was a fulfillment of that young promise. But the authenticity of the tale is suspect among Lincoln scholars. John Hanks recalled it thirty-five years afterward as a personal witness, whereas, according to Lincoln, Hanks had not gone beyond St. Louis on the journey. Beveridge observes that Lincoln himself apparently never spoke of the alleged incident publicly or privately, and that for twenty years afterward he showed little concern over slavery. We know that he refused to denounce the Fugitive Slave Law, viciously unfair though it was, even to free Negroes charged as runaways. ("I confess I hate to see the poor creatures hunted down," he wrote to Speed, ". . . but I bite my lips and keep quiet.")

His later career as an opponent of slavery extension must be interpreted in the light of his earlier public indifference to the question. Always moderately hostile to the South's "peculiar institution," he quieted himself with the comfortable thought that it was destined very gradually to disappear. Only after the Kansas-Nebraska Act breathed political life into the slavery issue did he seize upon it as a subject for agitation; only then did he attack it openly. His attitude was based on justice tempered by expediency — or perhaps more accurately, expediency tempered by justice.

Lincoln was by birth a Southerner, a Kentuckian; both his parents were Virginians. His father had served on the slave patrol of Hardin County. The Lincoln family was one of thousands that in the early decades of the nineteenth century had moved from the Southern states, particularly Virginia, Kentucky, and Tennessee, into the Valley of Democracy, and peopled the southern parts of Ohio, Indiana, and Illinois.

During his boyhood days in Indiana and Illinois Lincoln lived in communities where slaves were rare or unknown, and the problem was not thrust upon him. The prevailing attitude toward Negroes in Illinois was intensely hostile. Severe laws against free Negroes and runaway slaves were in force when Lincoln went to the Springfield legislature, and there is no evidence of any popular movement to liberalize them. Lincoln's experiences with slavery on his journeys to New Orleans in 1828 and 1831 do not seem to have made an impression vivid enough to change his conduct. Always privately compassionate, in his public career and his legal practice he never made himself the advocate of unpopular reform movements.

While Lincoln was serving his second term in the Illinois legislature the slavery question was discussed throughout the country. Garrison had begun his agitation, and petitions to abolish slavery in the District of Columbia had begun to pour in upon Congress. State legislatures began to express themselves upon the matter. The Illinois legislature turned the subject over to a joint committee, of which Lincoln and his Sangamon County colleague, Dan Stone, were members. At twenty-eight Lincoln thus had occasion to review the whole slavery question on both sides. The committee reported proslavery resolutions, presently adopted, which praised the beneficent effects of white civilization upon African natives, cited the wretchedness of emancipated Negroes as proof of the folly of freedom, and denounced abolitionists.

Lincoln voted against these resolutions. Six weeks later — the delay resulted from a desire to alienate no one from the cause that then stood closest to his heart, the removal of the state capital from Vandalia to Springfield — he and Stone embodied their own opinions in a resolution that was entered in the Journal of the House and promptly forgotten. It read in part: "They [Lincoln and Stone] believe that the institution of slavery is founded on injustice and bad policy, but that the promulgation of abolition doctrines tends to increase

rather than abate its evils." (Which means, the later Lincoln might have said, that slavery is wrong but that proposing to do away with it is also wrong because it makes slavery worse.) They went on to say that while the Constitution does not permit Congress to abolish slavery in the states, Congress can do so in the District of Columbia — *but* this power should not be exercised unless at "the request of the people of the District." This statement breathes the fire of an uncompromising insistence upon moderation. Let it be noted, however, that it did represent a point of view faintly to the left of prevailing opinion. Lincoln had gone on record as saying not merely that slavery was "bad policy" but even that it was unjust; but he had done so without jeopardizing his all-important project to transfer the state capital to Springfield.

In 1845, not long before he entered Congress, Lincoln again had occasion to express himself on slavery, this time in a carefully phrased private letter to a political supporter who happened to be an abolitionist.

I hold it a paramount duty of us in the free States, due to the Union of the States, and perhaps to liberty itself (paradox though it may seem), to let the slavery of the other states alone; while, on the other hand, I hold it to be equally clear that we should never knowingly lend ourselves, directly or indirectly, to prevent that slavery from dying a natural death — to find new places for it to live in, when it can not longer exist in the old.

Throughout his political career he consistently held to this position.

After he had become a lame-duck Congressman, Lincoln introduced into Congress in January 1849 a resolution to instruct the Committee on the District of Columbia to report a bill abolishing slavery in the District. The bill provided that children born of slave mothers after January 1, 1850 should be freed and supported by their mothers' owners until of a certain age. District slaveholders who wanted to emancipate their slaves were to be compensated from the federal Treasury. Lincoln himself added a section requiring the municipal authorities of Washington and Georgetown to provide "active and efficient means" of arresting and restoring to their owners all fugitive slaves escaping into the District. (This was six years before he confessed that he hated "to see the poor creatures hunted down.") Years later, recalling this fugitive-slave provision, Wendell Phillips referred to Lincoln somewhat unfairly as "that slavehound from Illinois." The bill itself, although not passed, gave rise to a spirited debate on the morality of slavery, in which Lincoln took no part.

When Lincoln returned to active politics the slavery issue had come to occupy the central position on the American scene. Stephen Douglas and some of his colleagues in Congress had secured the passage of the Kansas-Nebraska Act, which, by opening some new territory, formally at least, to slavery, repealed the part of the thirty-four-year-old Missouri Compromise that barred slavery from territory north of 36°30′. The measure provoked a howl of opposition in the North and split Douglas's party. The Republican Party, built on opposition to the extension of slavery, began to emerge in small communities in the Northwest. Lincoln's ambitions and interests were aroused, and he proceeded to rehabilitate his political fortunes.

His strategy was simple and forceful. He carefully avoided issues like the tariff, internal improvements, the Know-Nothing mania, or prohibitionism, each of which would alienate important groups of voters. He took pains in all his speeches to stress that he was not an abolitionist and at the same time to stand on the sole program of opposing the extension of slavery. On October 4, 1854, at the age of forty-five, Lincoln *for the first time in his life* denounced slavery in public. In his speech delivered in the Hall of Representatives at Springfield (and later repeated at Peoria) he declared that he hated the current zeal for the spread of slavery: "I hate it because of the monstrous injustice of slavery itself." He went on to say that he had no prejudice against the people of the South. He appreciated their argument that it would be difficult to get rid of the institution "in any satisfactory way." "I surely will not blame them for not doing what I should not know how to do myself. If all earthly power were given me, I should not know what to do as to the existing institution. My first impulse would be to free all the slaves and send them to Liberia, to their own native land." But immediate colonization, he added, is manifestly impossible. The slaves might be freed and kept "among us as underlings." Would this really better their condition?

What next? Free them, and make them politically and socially our equals. *My own feelings will not admit of this*, and if mine would, we well know that those of the great mass of whites will not. Whether this feeling accords with justice and sound judgment is not the sole question, if indeed it is any part of it. A universal feeling, whether well or ill founded, cannot be safely disregarded.

And yet nothing could justify an attempt to carry slavery into territories now free, Lincoln emphasized. For slavery is unquestionably wrong. "The great mass of mankind," he said at Peoria, "consider slavery a great moral wrong. [This feeling] lies at the very foundation of their sense of justice, and it cannot be trifled with. . . . No statesman can safely disregard it." The last sentence was the key to Lincoln's growing radicalism. As a practical politician he was naturally very much concerned about those public sentiments which no statesman can safely disregard. It was impossible, he had learned, safely to disregard either the feeling that slavery is a moral wrong or the feeling — held by an even larger portion of the public — that Negroes must not be given political and social equality.

He had now struck the core of the Republican problem in the Northwest: how to find a formula to reconcile the two opposing points of view held by great numbers of white people in the North. Lincoln's success in 1860 was due in no small part to his ability to bridge the gap, a performance that entitles him to a place among the world's great political propagandists.

To comprehend Lincoln's strategy we must keep one salient fact in mind: the abolitionists and their humanitarian sympathizers in the nation at large and particularly in the Northwest, the seat of Lincoln's strength, although numerous enough to hold the balance of power, were far too few to make a successful political party. Most of the white people of the Northwest, moreover, were in fact not only not abolitionists, but actually — and here is the core of the matter — Negrophobes. They feared and detested the very thought of living side by side with large numbers of Negroes in their own states, to say nothing of competing with their labor. Hence the severe laws against free Negroes, for example in Lincoln's Illinois. Amid all the agitation in Kansas over making the territory a free state, the conduct of the majority of

Republicans there was colored far more by self-interest than by moral principle. In their so-called Topeka Constitution the Kansas Republicans *forbade free Negroes even to come into the state,* and gave only to whites and Indians the right to vote. It was not bondage that troubled them — it was the Negro, free or slave. Again and again the Republican press of the Northwest referred to the Republican Party as the "White Man's Party." The motto of the leading Republican paper of Missouri, Frank Blair's *Daily Missouri Democrat,* was "White Men for Missouri and Missouri for White Men." Nothing could be more devastating to the contention that the early Republican Party in the Northwest was built upon moral principle. At the party convention of 1860 a plank endorsing the Declaration of Independence was almost hissed down and was saved only by the threat of a bolt by the antislavery element.

If the Republicans were to succeed in the strategic Northwest, how were they to win the support of both Negrophobes and antislavery men? Merely to insist that slavery was an evil would sound like abolitionism and offend the Negrophobes. Yet pitching their opposition to slavery extension on too low a moral level might lose the valued support of the humanitarians. Lincoln, perhaps borrowing from the old free-soil ideology, had the right formula and exploited it. He first hinted at it in the Peoria speech:

The whole nation is interested that the best use shall be made of these Territories. *We want them for homes of free white people. This they cannot be, to any considerable extent, if slavery shall be planted within them.* Slave States are places for poor white people to remove from, not to remove to. New free States are the places for poor people to go to, and better their condition. For this use the nation needs these Territories.

The full possibilities of this line first became clear in Lincoln's "lost" Bloomington speech, delivered at a Republican state convention in May 1856. There, according to the report of one of his colleagues at the Illinois bar, Lincoln warned that Douglas and his followers would frighten men away from the very idea of freedom with their incessant mouthing of the red-herring epithet: "Abolitionist!" "If that trick should succeed," he is reported to have said, "if free negroes should be made *things*, how long, think you, before they will begin to make *things* out of poor white men?"

Here was the answer to the Republican problem. Negrophobes and abolitionists alike could understand this threat; if freedom should be broken down they might themselves have to compete with the labor of slaves in the then free states — or might even be reduced to bondage along with the blacks! Here was an argument that could strike a responsive chord in the nervous system of every Northern man, farmer or worker, abolitionist or racist: *if a stop was not put somewhere upon the spread of slavery, the institution would become nation-wide.* Here, too, is the practical significance of the repeated statements Lincoln made in favor of labor at this time. Lincoln took the slavery question out of the realm of moral and legal dispute and, by dramatizing it in terms of free labor's self-interest, gave it a universal appeal. To please the abolitionists he kept saying that slavery was an evil thing; but for the material benefit of all Northern white men he opposed its further extension.

The importance of this argument becomes increasingly clear when it is realized that Lincoln used it in every one of his recorded speeches from 1854 until he became the President-elect. He once declared in Kansas that preventing slavery from becoming a nation-wide institution "is *the purpose* of this organization [the Republican Party]." The argument had a great allure too for the immigrants who were moving in such great numbers into the Northwest. Speaking at Alton, in the heart of a county where more than fifty per cent of the population was foreign-born, Lincoln went out of his way to make it clear that he favored keeping the territories open not only for native Americans, "but as an outlet for *free white people* everywhere, the world over — in which Hans, and Baptiste, and Patrick, and all other men from all the world, may find new homes and better their condition in life."

During the debates with Douglas, Lincoln dwelt on the theme again and again, and added the charge that Douglas himself was involved in a Democratic "conspiracy . . . for the sole purpose of nationalizing slavery." Douglas and the Supreme Court (which a year before had handed down the Dred Scott decision) would soon have the American people "working in the traces that tend to make this one universal slave nation." Chief Justice Taney had declared that Congress did not have the constitutional power to exclude slavery from the territories. The next step, said Lincoln, would be

another Supreme Court decision, declaring that the Constitution of the United States does not permit a *State* to exclude slavery from its limits. . . . We shall lie down pleasantly, dreaming that the people of Missouri are on the verge of making their State free;

and we shall awake to the reality instead, that the Supreme Court has made Illinois a slave State.

So also the theme of the "House Divided" speech:

I do not expect the Union to be dissolved — I do not expect the House to fall — but I do expect it to cease to be divided. It will become all one thing or all the other. Either the opponents of slavery will arrest the further spread of it, and place it where the public mind shall rest in the belief that it is in the course of ultimate extinction; or its advocates will push it forward, till it shall become alike lawful in all the States, old as well as new, North as well as South.

Have we no tendency to the latter condition?

The last sentence is invariably omitted when this passage is quoted, perhaps because from a literary standpoint it is anticlimactic. But in Lincoln's mind — and, one may guess, in the minds of those who heard him — it was not anticlimactic, but essential. Lincoln was *not* emphasizing the necessity for abolition of slavery in the near future; he was emphasizing the immediate "danger" that slavery would become a nation-wide American institution if its geographical spread were not severely restricted at once.

Once this "House Divided" speech had been made, Lincoln had to spend a great deal of time explaining it, proving that he was not an abolitionist. These efforts, together with his strategy of appealing to abolitionists and Negrophobes at once, involved him in embarrassing contradictions. In northern Illinois he spoke in one vein before abolition-minded audiences, but farther south, where settlers of Southern extraction were dominant, he spoke in another. It is instructive to compare what he said about the Negro in Chicago with what he said in Charleston.

Chicago, July 10, 1858:

Let us discard all this quibbling about this man and the other man, this race and that race and the other race being inferior, and therefore they must be placed in an inferior position. Let us discard all these things, and unite as one people throughout this land, until we shall once more stand up declaring that all men are created equal.

Charleston, September 18, 1858:

I will say, then, that I am not, nor ever have been, in favor of bringing about in any way the social and political equality of the white and black races [applause]: that I am not, nor ever have been, in favor of making voters or jurors of negroes, nor of qualifying them to hold office, nor to intermarry with white people. . . .

And inasmuch as they cannot so live, while they do remain together there must be the position of superior and inferior, and I as much as any other man am in favor of having the superior position assigned to the white race.

It is not easy to decide whether the true Lincoln is the one who spoke in Chicago or the one who spoke in Charleston. Possibly the man devoutly believed each of the utterances at the time he delivered it; possibly his mind too was a house divided against itself. In any case it is easy to see in all this the behavior of a professional politician looking for votes.[1]

Douglas did what he could to use

[1] Lincoln was fond of asserting that the Declaration of Independence, when it said that all men are created equal, included the Negro. He believed the Negro was probably inferior to the white man, he kept repeating, but in his right to eat, without anyone's leave, the bread he earned by his own labor, the Negro was the equal of any white man. Still he was opposed to citizenship for the Negro. How any man could be expected

Lincoln's inconsistency against him. At Galesburg, with his opponent sitting on the platform behind him, he proclaimed: "I would despise myself if I thought that I was procuring your votes by concealing my opinions, and by avowing one set of principles in one part of the state, and a different set in another." Confronted by Douglas with these clashing utterances from his Chicago and Charleston speeches, Lincoln replied: "I have not supposed and do not now suppose, that there is any conflict whatever between them."

But this was politics — the premium was on strategy, not intellectual consistency — and the effectiveness of Lincoln's campaign is beyond dispute. In the ensuing elections the Republican candi-

to defend his right to enjoy the fruits of his labor without having the power to defend it through his vote, Lincoln did not say. In his Peoria speech he had himself said: "No man is good enough to govern another man, without that man's consent." In one of his magnificent private memoranda on slavery Lincoln argued that anyone who defends the moral right of slavery creates an ethic by which his own enslavement may be justified. ("Fragment on Slavery," 1854.) But the same reasoning applies to anyone who would deny the Negro citizenship. It is impossible to avoid the conclusion that so far as the Negro was concerned, Lincoln could not escape the moral insensitivity that is characteristic of the average white American.

dates carried a majority of the voters and elected their state officers for the first time. Douglas returned to the Senate only because the Democrats, who had skillfully gerrymandered the election districts, still held their majority in the state legislature. Lincoln had contributed greatly to welding old-line Whigs and antislavery men into an effective party, and his reputation was growing by leaps and bounds. What he had done was to pick out an issue — the alleged plan to extend slavery, the alleged danger that it would spread throughout the nation — which would turn attention from the disintegrating forces in the Republican Party to the great integrating force. He was keenly aware that the party was built out of extremely heterogeneous elements, frankly speaking of it in his "House Divided" speech as composed of "strange, discordant, and even hostile elements." In addition to abolitionists and Negrophobes, it united high- and low-tariff men, hard- and soft-money men, former Whigs and former Democrats embittered by old political fights, Maine-law prohibitionists and German tipplers, Know-Nothings and immigrants. Lincoln's was the masterful diplomacy to hold such a coalition together, carry it into power, and with it win a war.

Lincoln-Douglas: DEBATES ON THE SLAVERY QUESTION

Lincoln's program for dealing with the slavery question was forged in his Senatorial campaign against Stephen A. Douglas in 1858. In opposition to Douglas' effort to compromise the political questions dividing the North and South, Lincoln called for a clear resolution of the moral issues underlying the conflict. The famous Lincoln-Douglas debates of 1858 set the tone for the ensuing political battle in the North which culminated in the election of Lincoln in 1860. These excerpts from the debates reproduce some of the major issues in that controversy.

DOUGLAS. I appear before you to-day for the purpose of discussing the leading political topics which now agitate the public mind. By an arrangement between Mr. Lincoln and myself, we are present here to-day for the purpose of having a joint discussion as the representatives of the two great political parties of the State and Union, upon the principles in issue between these parties, and this vast concourse of people shows the deep feeling which pervades the public mind in regard to the questions dividing us.

Prior to 1854 this country was divided into two great political parties, known as the Whig and Democratic parties. Both were national and patriotic, advocating principles that were universal in their application. An old line Whig could proclaim his principles in Louisiana and Massachusetts alike. Whig principles had no boundary sectional line, they were not limited by the Ohio river, nor by the Potomac, nor by the line of the free and slave States, but applied and were proclaimed wherever the Constitution ruled or the American flag waved over the American soil. So it was, and so it is with the great Democratic party, which, from the days of Jefferson until this period, has proven itself to be the historic party of this nation. While the Whig and Democratic parties differed in regard to a bank, the tariff, distribution, the specie circular and the sub-treasury, they agreed on the great slavery question which now agitates the Union. I say that the Whig party and the Democratic party agreed on this slavery question while they differed on those matters of expediency to which I have referred. The Whig party and the Democratic party jointly adopted the Compromise measures of 1850 as the basis of a proper and just solution of this slavery question in all its forms. Clay was the great leader, with Webster on his right and Cass on his left, and sustained by the patriots in the Whig and Democratic ranks, who had devised and enacted the Compromise measures of 1850. . . .

Reprinted by permission from Roy P. Basler, ed., *The Collected Works of Abraham Lincoln* (New Brunswick, N. J.: Rutgers University Press, 1953), III, 1–3, 7–9, 11–19, 27–30, 113–117, 145–146, 179–181, 212–219, 254–257, 265–267, 274–275, 305–306, 308–309, 312–316.

During the session of Congress of 1853–'54, I introduced into the Senate of the United States a bill to organize the Territories of Kansas and Nebraska on that principle which had been adopted in the compromise measures of 1850, approved by the Whig party and the Democratic party in Illinois in 1851, and endorsed by the Whig party and the Democratic party in national convention in 1852. In order that there might be no misunderstanding in relation to the principle involved in the Kansas and Nebraska bill, I put forth the true intent and meaning of the act in these words: "It is the true intent and meaning of this act not to legislate slavery into any State or Territory, or to exclude it therefrom, but to leave the people thereof perfectly free to form and regulate their domestic institutions in their own way, subject only to the federal constitution." Thus, you see, that up to 1854, when the Kansas and Nebraska bill was brought into Congress for the purpose of carrying out the principles which both parties had up to that time endorsed and approved, there had been no division in this country in regard to that principle except the opposition of the abolitionists. In the House of Representatives of the Illinois Legislature, upon a resolution asserting that principle, every Whig and every Democrat in the House voted in the affirmative, and only four men voted against it, and those four were old line Abolitionists.

In 1854, Mr. Abraham Lincoln and Mr. Trumbull entered into an arrangement, one with the other, and each with his respective friends, to dissolve the old Whig party on the one hand, and to dissolve the old Democratic party on the other, and to connect the members of both into an Abolition party under the name and disguise of a Republican party. . . .

Having formed this new party for the benefit of deserters from Whiggery, and deserters from Democracy, and having laid down the Abolition platform which I have read, Lincoln now takes his stand and proclaims his Abolition doctrines. . . . Mr. Lincoln . . . says that this Government cannot endure permanently in the same condition in which it was made by its framers — divided into free and slave States. He says that it has existed for about seventy years thus divided, and yet he tells you that it cannot endure permanently on the same principles and in the same relative condition in which our fathers made it. Why can it not exist divided into free and slave States? Washington, Jefferson, Franklin, Madison, Hamilton, Jay, and the great men of that day, made this Government divided into free States and slave States, and left each State perfectly free to do as it pleased on the subject of slavery. Why can it not exist on the same principles on which our fathers made it? They knew when they framed the Constitution that in a country as wide and broad as this, with such a variety of climate, production and interest, the people necessarily required different laws and institutions in different localities. They knew that the laws and regulations which would suit the granite hills of New Hampshire would be unsuited to the rice plantations of South Carolina, and they, therefore, provided that each State should retain its own Legislature, and its own sovereignty with the full and complete power to do as it pleased within its own limits, in all that was local and not national. One of the reserved rights of the States, was the right to regulate the relations between Master and Servant, on the slavery question. At the time the Constitution was formed, there were thirteen States in the Union, twelve of which were slaveholding States and one a free State. Suppose this doctrine of uniformity preached by Mr. Lincoln, that the States should all be free or all be slave had prevailed and what would have been the result? Of course, the twelve slaveholding States would have overruled the one free Statè, and slavery would have been fastened by a Constitutional provision on every inch of the American Republic, instead of being left as our fathers wisely left it, to each State to decide for itself. Here I assert that uniformity in the local laws and institutions of the different States is neither possible or desirable. . . .

Now, my friends, if we will only act conscientiously and rigidly upon this great principle of popular sovereignty which guarantees to each State and Territory the right to do as it pleases on all things local and domestic instead of Congress interfering, we will continue at peace one with another. Why should Illinois be at war with Missouri, or Kentucky with Ohio, or Virginia with New York, merely because their institutions differ? Our fathers intended that our institutions should differ. They knew that the North and the South having different climates, productions and interests, required different institutions. This doctrine of Mr. Lincoln's of uniformity among the institutions of the different States is a new doctrine, never dreamed of by Washington, Madison, or the framers of this Government. Mr. Lincoln and the Republican party set themselves up as wiser than these men who made this government, which has flourished for seventy years under the principle of popular sovereignty, recognizing the right of each State to do as it pleased. Under that principle, we have grown from a nation of three or four millions to a nation of about thirty millions of people; we have crossed the Allegheny mountains and filled up the whole North West, turning the prairie into a garden, and building up churches and schools, thus spreading civilization and Christianity where before there was nothing but savage-barbarism. Under that principle we have become from a feeble nation, the most powerful on the face of the earth, and if we only adhere to that principle, we can go forward increasing in territory, in power, in strength and in glory until the Republic of America shall be the North Star that shall guide the friends of freedom throughout the civilized world. And why can we not adhere to the great principle of self-government, upon which our institutions were originally based. I believe that this new doctrine preached by Mr. Lincoln and his party will dissolve the Union if it succeeds. They are trying to array all the Northern States in one body against the South, to excite a sectional war between the free States and the slave States, in order that the one or the other may be driven to the wall. . . .

LINCOLN. When a man hears himself somewhat misrepresented, it provokes him — at least, I find it so with myself; but when the misrepresentation becomes very gross and palpable, it is more apt to amuse him. . . .

In regard to that general abolition tilt that Judge Douglas makes, I hope you will permit me to read a part of a printed speech that I made at Peoria in 1854. . . .

When southern people tell us they are no more responsible for the origin of slavery, than we; I acknowledge the fact. When it is said that the institution exists, and that it is very difficult to get rid of it, in any satisfactory way, I can understand and appreciate the saying. I surely will not blame them for not doing what I should not know how to do myself. If all earthly power were given me, I should not know what to do, as to the existing institution. My first impulse would be to free all the slaves, and send them to Liberia, — to their own native land. But a moment's reflection would convince me, that whatever of high hope, (as I think there is) there may be in this, in the long run, its sudden execution is impossible. If they were all landed there in a day, they would all perish in the next ten days; and there are not surplus shipping and surplus money enough in the world to carry them there in many times ten days. What then? Free them all, and keep them among us as underlings? Is it quite certain that this betters their condition? I think I would not hold one in slavery, at any rate; yet the point is not clear enough to me to denounce people upon. What next? Free them, and make them politically and socially, our equals? My own feelings will not admit of this; and if mine would, we well know that those of the great mass of white people will not. Whether this feeling accords with justice and sound judgment, is not the sole question, if indeed, it is any part of it. A universal feeling, whether well or ill-founded, can not be safely disregarded. We can not, then, make them equals. It does seem to me that systems of gradual emancipation might be adopted; but for their tardiness in this, I will not undertake to judge our brethren of the south.

When they remind us of their constitutional rights, I acknowledge them, not grudgingly, but fully, and fairly; and I would give them any legislation for the reclaiming of their fugitives, which should not, in its stringency, be more likely to carry a free man into slavery, than our ordinary criminal laws are to hang an innocent one.

But all this, to my judgment, furnishes no more excuse for permitting slavery to go into our own free territory, than it would for reviving the African slave trade by law. . . .

Now gentlemen, I don't want to read at any greater length, but this is the true complexion of all I have ever said in regard to the institution of slavery and the black race. This is the whole of it, and anything that argues me into his idea of perfect social and political equality with the negro, is but a specious and fantastic arrangement of words, by which a man can prove a horse chestnut to be a chestnut horse. I will say here, while upon this subject, that I have no purpose directly or indirectly to interfere with the institution of slavery in the States where it exists. I believe I have no lawful right to do so, and I have no inclination to do so. I have no purpose to introduce political and social equality between the white and the black races. There is a physical difference between the two, which in my judgment will probably forever forbid their living together upon the footing of perfect equality, and inasmuch as it becomes a necessity that there must be a difference, I, as well as Judge Douglas, am in favor of the race to which I belong, having the superior position. I have never said anything to the contrary, but I hold that notwithstanding all this, there is no reason in the world why the negro is not entitled to all the natural rights enumerated in the Declaration of Independence, the right to life, liberty and the pursuit of happiness. I hold that he is as much entitled to these as the white man. I agree with Judge Douglas he is not my equal in many respects — certainly not in color, perhaps not in moral or intellectual endowment. But in the right to eat the bread, without leave of anybody else, which his own hand earns, *he is my equal and the equal of*

Judge Douglas, and the equal of every living man. . . .

The great variety of the local institutions in the States, springing from the differences in the soil, differences in the face of the country, and in the climate, are bonds of Union. They do not make "a house divided against itself," but they make a house united. If they produce in one section of the country what is called for by the wants of another section, and this other section can supply the wants of the first, they are not matters of discord but bonds of union, true bonds of union. But can this question of slavery be considered as among *these* varieties in the institutions of the country? I leave it to you to say whether, in the history of our government, this institution of slavery has not always failed to be a bond of union, and, on the contrary, been an apple of discord and an element of division in the house. I ask you to consider whether, so long as the moral constitution of men's minds shall continue to be the same after this generation and assemblage shall sink into the grave and another race shall arise, with the same moral and intellectual development we have — whether, if that institution is standing in the same irritating position in which it now is, it will not continue an element of division? If so, then I have a right to say that in regard to this question, the Union is a house divided against itself, and when the Judge reminds me that I have often said to him that the institution of slavery has existed for eighty years in some states, and yet it does not exist in some others, I agree to the fact, and I account for it by looking at the position in which our fathers originally placed it — restricting it from the new Territories where it had not gone, and legislating to cut off its source by the

abrogation of the slave trade, thus putting the seal of legislation *against its spread.* The public mind *did* rest in the belief that it was in the course of ultimate extinction. But lately, I think — and in this I charge nothing on the Judge's motives — lately, I think, that he, and those acting with him have placed that institution on a new basis, which looks to the *perpetuity and nationalization of slavery.* And while it is placed upon this new basis, I say, and I have said, that I believe we shall not have peace upon the question until the opponents of slavery arrest the further spread of it, and place it where the public mind shall rest in the belief that it is in the course of ultimate extinction; or, on the other hand, that its advocates will push it forward until it shall become alike lawful in all the States, old as well as new, North as well as South. Now I believe if we could arrest the spread, and place it where Washington, and Jefferson, and Madison placed it, it *would be* in the course of ultimate extinction, and the public mind *would,* as for eighty years past, believe that it was in the course of ultimate extinction. The crisis would be past and the institution might be left alone for a hundred years, if it should live so long, in the States where it exists, yet it would be going out of existence in the way best for both the black and the white races.

A VOICE. Then do you repudiate Popular Sovereignty?

LINCOLN. Well, then, let us talk about Popular Sovereignty! What is Popular Sovereignty? Is it the right of the people to have Slavery or not have it, as they see fit, in the territories? I will state — and I have an able man to watch me — my understanding is that Popular Sovereignty, as now applied to the question of Slavery, does allow the people of a

Territory to have Slavery if they want to, but does not allow them *not* to have it if they *do not* want it. I do not mean that if this vast concourse of people were in a Territory of the United States, any one of them would be obliged to have a slave if he did not want one; but I do say that, as I understand the Dred Scott decision, if any one man wants slaves, all the rest have no way of keeping that one man from holding them. . . .

Then, what is necessary for the nationalization of slavery? It is simply the next Dred Scott decision. It is merely for the Supreme Court to decide that no *State* under the Constitution can exclude it, just as they have already decided that under the Constitution neither Congress nor the Territorial Legislature can do it. This being true, and this being the way as I think that slavery is to be made national, let us consider what Judge Douglas is doing every day to that end. In the first place, let us see what influence he is exerting on public sentiment. In this and like communities, public sentiment is everything. With public sentiment, nothing can fail; without it nothing can succeed. Consequently he who moulds public sentiment, goes deeper than he who enacts statutes or pronounces decisions. He makes statutes and decisions possible or impossible to be executed. This must be borne in mind as also the additional fact that Judge Douglas is a man of vast influence, so great that it is enough for many men to profess to believe anything, when they once find out that Judge Douglas professes to believe it. Consider also the attitude he occupies at the head of a large party — a party which he claims has a majority of all the voters in the country. This man sticks to a decision which forbids the people of a Territory from excluding slavery, and he does so not because he says it is right in itself

— he does not give an opinion on that — but because it has been decided by the court, and being *decided by the court*, he is, and you are bound to take it in your political action as *law* — not that he judges at all of its merits, but because a decision of the court is to him a "Thus saith the Lord." He places it on that ground alone, and you will bear in mind that thus committing himself unreservedly to this decision, *commits him to the next one* just as firmly as to this . . .

And now I will only say that when, by all these means and appliances Judge Douglas shall succeed in bringing public sentiment to an exact accordance with his own views — when these vast assemblages shall echo back all these sentiments — when they shall come to repeat his views and to avow his principles, and to say all that he says on these mighty questions — then it needs only the formality of the second Dred Scott decision, which he endorses in advance, to make Slavery alike lawful in all the States — old as well as new, North as well as South.

DOUGLAS. My friends, I am in favor of preserving this government as our fathers made it. It does not follow by any means that because a negro is not your equal or mine that hence he must necessarily be a slave. On the contrary, it does follow that we ought to extend to the negro every right, every privilege, every immunity which he is capable of enjoying consistent with the good of society. When you ask me what these rights are, what their nature and extent is, I tell you that that is a question which each State of this Union must decide for itself. Illinois has already decided the question. We have decided that the negro must not be a slave within our limits, but we have also decided that the negro shall not be a citizen within our limits; that he shall not vote, hold office, or exercise any political rights. I maintain that Illinois, as a sovereign State, has a right thus to fix her policy with reference to the relation between the white man and the negro; but while we had the right to decide the question for ourselves we must recognize the same right in Kentucky and in every other State to make the same decision, or a different one. Having decided our own policy with reference to the black race, we must leave Kentucky and Missouri and every other State perfectly free to make just such a decision as they see proper on that question. . . .

If we wish to preserve our institutions in their purity, and transmit them unimpaired to our latest posterity, we must preserve with religious good faith that great principle of self government which guarantees to each and every State, old and new, the right to make just such constitutions as they deserve, and come into the Union with their own constitution and not one palmed upon them. Whenever you sanction the doctrine that Congress may crowd a constitution down the throats of an unwilling people against their consent, you will subvert the great fundamental principle upon which all our free institutions rest. In the future I have no fear that the attempt will ever be made. President Buchanan declared in his annual message, that hereafter the rule adopted in the Minnesota case, requiring a constitution to be submitted to the people, should be followed in all future cases, and if he stands by that recommendation there will be no division in the Democratic party on that principle in the future. Hence, the great mission of the Democracy is to unite the fraternal feeling of the whole country, restore peace and quiet by teaching each

State to mind its own business, and regulate its own domestic affairs, and all to unite carrying out the constitution as our fathers made it, and thus to preserve the Union and render it perpetual in all time to come. Why should we not act as our fathers who made the government? There was no sectional strife in Washington's army. They were all brethren of a common confederacy, they fought under a common flag that they might bestow upon their posterity a common destiny, and to this end they poured out their blood in common streams and shared in some instances a common grave.

LINCOLN. There is very much in the principles that Judge Douglas has here enunciated that I most cordially approve, and over which I shall have no controversy with him. In so far as he has insisted that all the States have the right to do exactly as they please about all their domestic relations, including that of slavery, I agree entirely with him. He places me wrong in spite of all I can tell him, though I repeat it again and again, insisting that I have no difference with him upon this subject. I have made a great many speeches, some of which have been printed, and it will be utterly impossible for him to find anything that I have ever put in print contrary to what I now say upon this subject. I hold myself under constitutional obligations to allow the people in all the States without interference, direct or indirect, to do exactly as they please, and I deny that I have any inclination to interfere with them, even if there were no such constitutional obligation. I can only say again that I am placed improperly — altogether improperly in spite of all I can say — when it is insisted that I entertain any other view or purposes in regard to that matter.

While I am upon this subject, I will make some answers briefly to certain propositions that Judge Douglas has put. He says, "Why can't this Union endure permanently, half slave and half free?" I have said that I supposed it could not, and I will try, before this new audience, to give briefly some of the reasons for entertaining that opinion. Another form of his question is, "Why can't we let it stand as our fathers placed it?" That is the exact difficulty between us, I say that Judge Douglas and his friends have changed them from the position in which our fathers originally placed it. I say in the way our fathers originally left the slavery question, the institution was in the course of ultimate extinction, and the public mind rested in the belief that it *was* in the course of ultimate extinction. I say when this government was first established it was the policy of its founders to prohibit the spread of slavery into the new Territories of the United States, where it had not existed. But Judge Douglas and his friends have broken up that policy and placed it upon a new basis by which it is to become national and perpetual. All I have asked or desired anywhere is that it should be placed back again upon the basis that the fathers of our government originally placed it upon. I have no doubt that it *would* become extinct, for all time to come, if we but re-adopted the policy of the fathers by restricting it to the limits it has already covered — restricting it from the new Territories. . . .

While I was at the hotel to-day an elderly gentleman called upon me to know whether I was really in favor of producing a perfect equality between the negroes and white people. While I had not proposed to myself on this occasion to say much on that subject, yet as the question was asked me I thought I would occupy perhaps five minutes in saying something in regard to it. I will say then that I am not, nor ever have been in favor of bringing about in any way the social and political equality of the white and black races, — that I am not nor ever have been in favor of making voters or jurors of negroes, nor of qualifying them to hold office, nor to intermarry with white people; and I will say in addition to this that there is a physical difference between the white and black races which I believe will for ever forbid the two races living together on terms of social and political equality. And inasmuch as they cannot so live, while they do remain together there must be the position of superior and inferior, and I as much as any other man am in favor of having the superior position assigned to the white race. I say upon this occasion I do not perceive that because the white man is to have the superior position the negro should be denied everything. I do not understand that because I do not want a negro woman for a slave I must necessarily want her for a wife. My understanding is that I can just let her alone. I am now in my fiftieth year, and I certainly never have had a black woman for either a slave or a wife. So it seems to me quite possible for us to get along without making either slaves or wives of negroes. . . .

Judge Douglas has said to you that he has not been able to get from me an answer to the question whether I am in favor of negro-citizenship. So far as I know, the Judge never asked me the question before. He shall have no occasion to ever ask it again, for I tell him very frankly that I am not in favor of negro citizenship. . . . Now my opinion is that the different States have the power to make a negro a citizen under the Constitution of the United States if they choose. The Dred Scott decision decides that they have not that power. If the State of Illinois had that power I should be opposed to the exercise of it. That is all I have to say about it.

. . . While I am here perhaps I ought to say a word, if I have the time, in regard to the latter portion of the Judge's speech, which was a sort of declamation in reference to my having said I entertained the belief that this government would not endure, half slave and half free. I have said so and I did not say it without what seemed to me to be good reasons. It perhaps would require more time than I have now to set forth these reasons in detail; but let me ask you a few questions. Have we ever had any peace on this slavery question? When are we to have peace upon it if it is kept in the position it now occupies? How are we ever to have peace upon it? . . . I say, then, there is no way of putting an end to the slavery agitation amongst us but to put it back upon the basis where our fathers placed it, no way but to keep it out of our new Territories — to restrict it forever to the old States where it now exists. Then the public mind *will* rest in the belief that it is in the course of ultimate extinction. That is one way of putting an end to the slavery agitation.

The other way is for us to surrender and let Judge Douglas and his friends have their way and plant slavery over all the States — cease speaking of it as in any way a wrong — regard slavery as one of the common matters of property, and speak of negroes as we do of our horses and cattle. But while it drives on in its state of progress as it is now driving, and as it has driven for the last five years, I have ventured the opinion, and I say today, that we will have no end to the slavery agitation until it takes one turn or the other. I do not mean that when it

takes a turn towards ultimate extinction it will be in a day, nor in a year, nor in two years. I do not suppose that in the most peaceful way ultimate extinction would occur in less than a hundred years at the least; but that it will occur in the best way for both races in God's own good time, I have no doubt. . . .

DOUGLAS. Now, let me ask you whether the country has any interest in sustaining this organization known as the Republican party? That party is unlike all other political organizations in this country. All other parties have been national in their character — have avowed their principles alike in the slave and the free States, in Kentucky as well as in Illinois, in Louisiana as well as in Massachusetts. Such was the case with the old Whig party, and such was and is the case with the Democratic party. Whigs and Democrats could proclaim their principles boldly and fearlessly in the north and in the south, in the east and in the west, wherever the constitution ruled and the American flag waved over American soil.

But now you have a sectional organization, a party which appeals to the northern section of the Union against the southern, a party which appeals to northern passion, northern pride, northern ambition, and northern prejudices, against southern people, the southern States and southern institutions. The leaders of that party hope that they will be able to unite the northern States in one great sectional party, and inasmuch as the North is the strongest section, that they will thus be enabled to outvote, conquer, govern, and control the South. Hence you find that they now make speeches advocating principles and measures which cannot be defended in any slave-holding State of this Union. Is there a Republican residing in Galesburg who can travel into

Kentucky and carry his principles with him across the Ohio? What Republican from Massachusetts can visit the Old Dominion without leaving his principles behind him when he crosses Mason and Dixon's line? Permit me to say to you in perfect good humor, but in all sincerity, that no political creed is sound which cannot be proclaimed fearlessly in every State of this Union where the Federal Constitution is not the supreme law of the land. Not only is this Republican party unable to proclaim its principles alike in the North and in the South, in the free States and in the slave States, but it cannot even proclaim them in the same forms and give them the same strength and meaning in all parts of the same State. My friend Lincoln finds it extremely difficult to manage a debate in the centre part of the State, where there is a mixture of men from the North and the South. In the extreme northern part of Illinois he can proclaim as bold and radical abolitionism as ever Giddings, Lovejoy, or Garrison enunciated, but when he gets down a little further South he claims that he is an old line Whig, a disciple of Henry Clay, and declares that he still adheres to the old line Whig creed, and has nothing whatever to do with Abolitionism, or negro equality, or negro citizenship. I once before hinted this of Mr. Lincoln in a public speech, and at Charleston he defied me to show that there was any difference between his speeches in the North and in the South, and that they were not in strict harmony. I will now call your attention to two of them, and you can then say whether you would be apt to believe that the same man ever uttered both. In a speech in reply to me at Chicago in July last, Mr. Lincoln, in speaking of the equality of the negro with the white man used the following language:

My friends, [he says,] I have detained you about as long as I desire to do, and I have only to say let us discard all this quibbling about this man and the other man — this race and that race, and the other race being inferior and therefore they must be placed in an inferior position, discarding our standard that we have left us. Let us discard all these things, and unite as one people throughout this land, until we shall once more stand up declaring that all men are created equal.

. . . I will show you in immediate contrast with that doctrine, what Mr. Lincoln said down in Egypt in order to get votes in that locality where they do not hold to such a doctrine. In a joint discussion between Mr. Lincoln and myself, at Charleston, I think, on the 18th of last month, Mr. Lincoln referring to this subject used the following language:

I will say then, that I am not nor never have been in favor of bringing about in any way, the social and political equality of the white and black races; that I am not nor never have been in favor of making voters of the free negroes, or jurors, or qualifying them to hold office, or having them to marry with white people. I will say in addition, that there is a physical difference between the white and black races, which, I suppose, will forever forbid the two races living together upon terms of social and political equality, and inasmuch as they cannot so live, that while they do remain together, there must be the position of superior and inferior, that I as much as any other white man am in favor of the superior position being assigned to the white man.

. . . Abolitionists up north are expected and required to vote for Lincoln because he goes for the equality of the races, holding that by the Declaration of Independence the white man and the negro were created equal and endowed by the

Divine law with that equality, and down south he tells the old Whigs, the Kentuckians, Virginians, and Tennesseeans, that there is a physical difference in the races, making one superior and the other inferior, and that he is in favor of maintaining the superiority of the white race over the negro. Now, how can you reconcile those two positions of Mr. Lincoln? He is to be voted for in the south as a pro-slavery man, and he is to be voted for in the north as an Abolitionist. Up here he thinks it is all nonsense to talk about a difference between the races, and says that we must "discard all quibbling about this race and that race and the other race being inferior, and therefore they must be placed in an inferior position." Down south he makes this "quibble" about this race and that race and the other race being inferior as the creed of his party, and declares that the negro can never be elevated to the position of the white man. . . . Thus you find that Mr. Lincoln's creed cannot travel through even one half of the counties of this State, but that it changes its hues and becomes lighter and lighter, as it travels from the extreme North, until it is nearly white, when it reaches the extreme south end of the State. I ask you, my friends, why cannot Republicans avow their principles alike everywhere? I would despise myself if I thought that I was procuring your votes by concealing my opinions, and by avowing one set of principles in one part of the State, and a different set in another part. If I do not truly and honorably represent your feelings and principles, then I ought not to be your Senator; and I will never conceal my opinions, or modify or change them a hair's breadth in order to get votes. . . . The great principle of this government is that each State has the right to do as it pleases on all these questions, and no other State, or power on earth has the right to interfere with us, or complain of us merely because our system differs from theirs. In the compromise measures of 1850, Mr. Clay declared that this great principle ought to exist in the territories as well as in the States, and I reasserted his doctrine in the Kansas and Nebraska bill in 1854.

But Mr. Lincoln cannot be made to understand, and those who are determined to vote for him, no matter whether he is a pro-slavery man in the south and a negro equality advocate in the north, cannot be made to understand how it is that in a territory the people can do as they please on the slavery question under the Dred Scott decision. Let us see whether I cannot explain it to the satisfaction of all impartial men. Chief Justice Taney has said in his opinion in the Dred Scott case, that a negro slave being property, stands on an equal footing with other property, and that the owner may carry them into United States territory the same as he does other property. Suppose any two of you, neighbors, should conclude to go to Kansas, one carrying $100,000 worth of negro slaves and the other $100,000 worth of mixed merchandise, including quantities of liquors. You both agree that under that decision you may carry your property to Kansas, but when you get it there, the merchant who is possessed of the liquors is met by the Maine liquor law, which prohibits the sale or use of his property, and the owner of the slaves is met by equally unfriendly legislation, which makes his property worthless after he gets it there. What is the right to carry your property into the territory worth to either, when unfriendly legislation in the territory renders it worthless after you get it there? The slaveholder when he gets his slaves there finds that there is no local law to protect him in holding them, no slave code, no police regulation maintaining and supporting him in his right, and he discovers at once that the absence of such friendly legislation excludes his property from the territory, just as irresistibly as if there was a positive constitutional prohibition excluding it. Thus you find it is with any kind of property in a territory, it depends for its protection on the local and municipal law. If the people of a territory want slavery, they make friendly legislation to introduce it, but if they do not want it, they withhold all protection from it, and then it cannot exist there. . . . I hold that in this country there is no power on the face of the globe that can force any institution on an unwilling people. The great fundamental principle of our government is that the people of each State and each territory shall be left perfectly free to decide for themselves what shall be the nature and character of their institutions. When this government was made, it was based on that principle. At the time of its formation there were twelve slaveholding States and one free State in this Union. Suppose this doctrine of Mr. Lincoln and the Republicans, of uniformity of the laws of all the States on the subject of slavery, had prevailed; suppose Mr. Lincoln himself had been a member of the convention which framed the constitution, and that he had risen in that august body, and addressing the father of his country, had said as he did at Springfield:

A house divided against itself cannot stand. I believe this government cannot endure permanently half slave and half free. I do not expect the Union to be dissolved — I do not expect the house to fall, but I do expect it will cease to be divided. It will become all one thing or all the other.

What do you think would have been the result? Suppose he had made that convention believe that doctrine and they had acted upon it, what do you think would have been the result? Do you believe that the one free State would have outvoted the twelve slaveholding States, and thus abolished slavery? On the contrary, would not the twelve slaveholding States have outvoted the one free State, and under his doctrine have fastened slavery by an irrevocable constitutional provision upon every inch of the American Republic? Thus you see that the doctrine he now advocates, if proclaimed at the beginning of the government, would have established slavery everywhere throughout the American continent, and are you willing, now that we have the majority section, to exercise a power which we never would have submitted to when we were in the minority? If the Southern States had attempted to control our institutions, and make the States all slave when they had the power, I ask would you have submitted to it? If you would not, are you willing now that we have become the strongest under that great principle of self-government that allows each State to do as it pleases — to attempt to control the Southern institutions? Then, my friends, I say to you that there is but one path of peace in this republic, and that is to administer this government as our fathers made it, divided into free and slave States, allowing each State to decide for itself whether it wants slavery or not. If Illinois will settle the slavery question for herself, mind her own business and let her neighbors alone, we will be at peace with Kentucky, and every other Southern State. If every other State in the Union will do the same there will be peace between the North and the South, and in the whole Union.

LINCOLN. We have in this nation this element of domestic slavery. It is a matter of absolute certainty that it is a disturbing element. It is the opinion of all the great men who have expressed an opinion upon it, that it is a dangerous element. We keep up a controversy in regard to it. That controversy necessarily springs from difference of opinion, and if we can learn exactly — can reduce to the lowest elements — what that difference of opinion is, we perhaps shall be better prepared for discussing the different systems of policy that we would propose in regard to that disturbing element. I suggest that the difference of opinion, reduced to its lowest terms, is no other than the difference between the men who think slavery a wrong and those who do not think it wrong. The Republican party think it wrong — we think it is a moral, a social and a political wrong. We think it is a wrong not confining itself merely to the persons or the States where it exists, but that it is a wrong in its tendency, to say the least, that extends itself to the existence of the whole nation. Because we think it wrong, we propose a course of policy that shall deal with it as a wrong. We deal with it as with any other wrong, in so far as we can prevent its growing any larger, and so deal with it that in the run of time there may be some promise of an end to it. We have a due regard to the actual presence of it amongst us and the difficulties of getting rid of it in any satisfactory way, and all the constitutional obligations thrown about it. I suppose that in reference both to its actual existence in the nation, and to our constitutional obligations, we have no right at all to disturb it in the States where it exists, and we profess that we have no more inclination to disturb it than we have the right to do it. We go further than that; we don't propose to disturb it where, in one instance, we think the Constitution would permit us. We think the Constitution would permit us to disturb it in the District of Columbia. Still we do not propose to do that, unless it should be in terms which I don't suppose the nation is very likely soon to agree to — the terms of making the emancipation gradual and compensating the unwilling owners. Where we suppose we have the constitutional right, we restrain ourselves in reference to the actual existence of the institution and the difficulties thrown about it. We also oppose it as an evil so far as it seeks to spread itself. We insist on the policy that shall restrict it to its present limits. We don't suppose that in doing this we violate anything due to the actual presence of the institution, or anything due to the constitutional guarantees thrown around it.

We oppose the Dred Scott decision in a certain way, upon which I ought perhaps to address you a few words. We do not propose that when Dred Scott has been decided to be a slave by the court, we, as a mob, will decide him to be free. We do not propose that, when any other one, or one thousand, shall be decided by that court to be slaves, we will in any violent way disturb the rights of property thus settled; but we nevertheless do oppose that decision as a political rule which shall be binding on the voter, to vote for nobody who thinks it wrong, which shall be binding on the members of Congress or the President to favor no measure that does not actually concur with the principles of that decision. We do not propose to be bound by it as a political rule in that way, because we think it lays the foundation not merely of enlarging and spreading out what we consider an evil, but it lays the foundation for spreading that evil into the States themselves. We propose so resisting it as to have it reversed if we can, and a new judicial rule established upon this subject.

I will add this, that if there be any man who does not believe that slavery is wrong in the three aspects which I have mentioned, or in any one of them, that man is misplaced, and ought to leave us. While, on the other hand, if there be any man in the Republican party who is impatient over the necessity springing from its actual presence, and is impatient of the constitutional guarantees thrown around it, and would act in disregard of these, he too is misplaced standing with us. He will find his place somewhere else; for we have a due regard, so far as we are capable of understanding them, for all these things. This, gentlemen, as well as I can give it, is a plain statement of our principles in all their enormity.

I will say now that there is a sentiment in the country contrary to me — a sentiment which holds that slavery is not wrong, and therefore it goes for policy that does not propose dealing with it as a wrong. That policy is the Democratic policy, and that sentiment is the Democratic sentiment. If there be a doubt in the mind of any one of this vast audience that this is really the central idea of the Democratic party, in relation to this subject, I ask him to bear with me while I state a few things tending, as I think, to prove that proposition. In the first place, the leading man — I think I may do my friend Judge Douglas the honor of calling him such — advocating the present Democratic policy, never himself says it is wrong. He has the high distinction, so far as I know, of never having said slavery is either right or wrong. Almost everybody else says one or the other, but the Judge never does. If there be a man in the Democratic party who thinks it is

wrong, and yet clings to that party, I suggest to him in the first place that his leader don't talk as he does, for he never says that it is wrong. In the second place, I suggest to him that if he will examine the policy proposed to be carried forward, he will find that he carefully excludes the idea that there is anything wrong in it. If you will examine the arguments that are made on it, you will find that every one carefully excludes the idea that there is anything wrong in slavery. Perhaps that Democrat who says he is as much opposed to slavery as I am, will tell me that I am wrong about this. I wish him to examine his own course in regard to this matter a moment, and then see if his opinion will not be changed a little. You say it is wrong; but don't you constantly object to anybody else saying so? Do you not constantly argue that this is not the right place to oppose it? You say it must not be opposed in the free States, because slavery is not here; it must not be opposed in the slave States, because it is there; it must not be opposed in politics, because that will make a fuss; it must not be opposed in the pulpit, because it is not religion. Then where is the place to oppose it? There is no suitable place to oppose it. There is no place in the country to oppose this evil overspreading the continent, which you say yourself is coming. Frank Blair and Gratz Brown tried to get up a system of gradual emancipation in Missouri, had an election in August and got beat, and you, Mr. Democrat, threw up your hat, and halloed "hurrah for Democracy." So I say again that in regard to the arguments that are made, when Judge Douglas says he "don't care whether slavery is voted up or voted down," whether he means that as an individual expression of sentiment, or only as a sort of statement of his views on national policy, it is alike true to say that he can thus argue logically if he don't see anything wrong in it; but he cannot say so logically if he admits that slavery is wrong. He cannot say that he would as soon see a wrong voted up as voted down. When Judge Douglas says that whoever, or whatever community, wants slaves, they have a right to have them, he is perfectly logical if there is nothing wrong in the institution; but if you admit that it is wrong, he cannot logically say that anybody has a right to do wrong. When he says that slave property and horse and hog property are alike to be allowed to go into the Territories, upon the principles of equality, he is reasoning truly, if there is no difference between them as property; but if the one is property, held rightfully, and the other is wrong, then there is no equality between the right and wrong; so that, turn it in any way you can, in all the arguments sustaining the Democratic policy, and in that policy itself, there is a careful, studied exclusion of the idea that there is anything wrong in slavery. Let us understand this. I am not, just here, trying to prove that we are right and they are wrong. I have been stating where we and they stand, and trying to show what is the real difference between us; and I now say that whenever we can get the question distinctly stated — can get all these men who believe that slavery is in some of these respects wrong, to stand and act with us in treating it as a wrong — then, and not till then, I think we will in some way come to an end of this slavery agitation.

❧ DOUGLAS. Mr. Lincoln thinks that it is his duty to preach a crusade in the free States, against slavery, because it is a crime, as he believes, and ought to be extinguished; and because the people of the slave States will never abolish it. How is he going to abolish it? Down in the southern part of the State he takes the ground openly that he will not interfere with slavery where it exists, and says that he is not now and never was in favor of interfering with slavery where it exists in the States. Well, if he is not in favor of that, how does he expect to bring slavery in a course of ultimate extinction? How can he extinguish it in Kentucky, in Virginia, in all the slave States by his policy, if he will not pursue a policy which will interfere with it in the States where it exists? . . .

Mr. Lincoln there [at Springfield before the Republican convention] told his Abolition friends that this government could not endure permanently, divided into free and slave States as our fathers made it, and that it must become all free or all slave, otherwise, that the government could not exist. How then does Lincoln propose to save the Union, unless by compelling all the States to become free, so that the house shall not be divided against itself? He intends making them all free; he will preserve the Union in that way, and yet, he is not going to interfere with slavery anywhere it now exists. How is he going to bring it about? . . .

He tells you that I will not argue the question whether slavery is right or wrong. I tell you why I will not do it. I hold that under the Constitution of the United States, each State of this Union has a right to do as it pleases on the subject of slavery. In Illinois we have exercised that sovereign right by prohibiting slavery within our own limits. I approve of that line of policy. We have performed our whole duty in Illinois. We have gone as far as we have a right to go under the constitution of our common country. It is none of our business whether slavery exists in Missouri or not. Missouri is a sovereign State of this Union, and has the same right to decide the slavery question for herself that Illinois has to decide it for herself. Hence I do not choose to occupy the time allotted to me in discussing a question that we have no right to act upon. I thought that you desired to hear us upon those questions coming within our constitutional power of action. Lincoln will not discuss these. What one question has he discussed that comes within the power or calls for the action or interference of an United States Senator? He is going to discuss the rightfulness of slavery when Congress cannot act upon it either way. He wishes to discuss the merits of the Dred Scott decision when under the constitution, a Senator has no right to interfere with the decision of judicial tribunals. He wants your exclusive attention to two questions that he has no power to act upon; to two questions that he could not vote upon if he was in Congress, to two questions that are not practical, in order to conceal your attention from other questions which he might be required to vote upon should he ever become a member of Congress. He tells you that he does not like the Dred Scott decision. Suppose he does not, how is he going to help himself? He says that he will reverse it. How will he reverse it? I know of but one mode of reversing judicial decisions, and that is by appealing from the inferior to the superior court. But I have never yet learned how or where an appeal could be taken from the Supreme Court of the United States! The Dred Scott decision was pronounced by the highest tribunal on earth. From that decision there is no appeal this side of Heaven. Yet, Mr. Lincoln says he is going to reverse that decision. By what tribunal will he reverse it? Will he appeal to a mob? Does he intend to appeal to violence, to Lynch law? Will he stir up strife and rebellion in the land and overthrow the court by violence? He does not deign to tell you how he will reverse the Dred Scott decision, but keeps appealing each day from the Supreme Court of the United States to political meetings in the country. He wants me to argue with you the merits of each point of that decision before this political meeting. I say to you, with all due respect, that I choose to abide by the decisions of the Supreme Court as they are pronounced. It is not for me to inquire after a decision is made whether I like it in all the points or not. When I used to practice law with Lincoln, I never knew him to be beat in a case that he did not get mad at the judge and talk about appealing; and when I got beat I generally thought the court was wrong, but I never dreamed of going out of the court house and making a stump speech to the people against the judge, merely because I had found out that I did not know the law as well as he did. If the decision did not suit me, I appealed until I got to the Supreme Court, and then if that court, the highest tribunal in the world, decided against me, I was satisfied, because it is the duty of every law-abiding man to obey the constitutions, the laws, and the constituted authorities. He who attempts to stir up odium and rebellion in the country against the constituted authorities, is stimulating the passions of men to resort to violence and to mobs instead of to the law. Hence, I tell you that I take the decisions of the Supreme Court as the law of the land, and I intend to obey them as such. . . .

If each State will only agree to mind its own business, and let its neighbors alone, there will be peace forever between us. We in Illinois tried slavery when a territory, and found it was not good for us in this climate and with our surroundings, and hence we abolished it. We then adopted a free State constitution, as we had a right to do. In this State we have declared that a negro shall not be a citizen, and we have also declared that he shall not be a slave. We had a right to adopt that policy. Missouri has just as good a right to adopt the other policy. I am now speaking of rights under the constitution, and not of moral or religious rights. I do not discuss the morals of the people of Missouri, but let them settle that matter for themselves. I hold that the people of the slaveholding States are civilized men as well as ourselves, that they bear consciences as well as we, and that they are accountable to God and their posterity and not to us. It is for them to decide therefore the moral and religious right of the slavery question for themselves within their own limits. I assert that they had as much right under the constitution to adopt the system of policy which they have as we had to adopt ours. So it is with every other State in this Union. Let each State stand firmly by that great constitutional right, let each State mind its own business and let its neighbors alone, and there will be no trouble on this question. If we will stand by that principle, then Mr. Lincoln will find that this republic can exist forever divided into free and slave States, as our fathers made it and the people of each State have decided. Stand by that great principle and we can go on as we have done, increasing in wealth, in population, in power, and in all the elements of greatness, until we shall be the admiration and terror of the world. We can go on and enlarge as our population increases, and we require more room, until we make this continent one ocean-bound republic. Under that principle the United States can perform that great mission, that destiny which Providence has marked out for us. Under that principle we can receive with entire safety that stream of intelligence which is constantly flowing from the Old World to the New, filling up our prairies, clearing our wildernesses and building cities, towns, railroads and other internal improvements, and thus make this the asylum of the oppressed of the whole earth. We have this great mission to perform, and it can only be performed by adhering faithfully to that principle of self-government on which our institutions were all established. I repeat that the principle is the right of each State, each territory, to decide this slavery question for itself, to have slavery or not, as it chooses, and it does not become Mr. Lincoln, or anybody else, to tell the people of Kentucky that they have no consciences, that they are living in a state of iniquity, and that they are cherishing an institution to their bosoms in violation of the law of God. Better for him to adopt the doctrine of "judge not lest ye be judged." Let him perform his own duty at home, and he will have a better fate in the future. I think there are objects of charity enough in the free States to excite the sympathies and open the pockets of all the benevolence we have amongst us, without going abroad in search of negroes, of whose condition we know nothing. We have enough objects of charity at home, and it is our duty to take care of our own poor, and our own suffering, before we go abroad to intermeddle with other people's business. . . .

LINCOLN. Judge Douglas has again referred to a Springfield speech in which I said "a house divided against itself cannot stand.". . . That extract and the sentiments expressed in it, have been extremely offensive to Judge Douglas. He has warred upon them as Satan does upon the Bible. His perversions upon it are endless. Here now are my views upon it in brief.

I have intimated that I thought the agitation would not cease until a crisis should have been reached and passed. I have stated in what way I thought it would be reached and passed. I have said that it might go one way or the other. We might, by arresting the further spread of it and placing it where the fathers originally placed it, put it where the public mind should rest in the belief that it was in the course of ultimate extinction. Thus the agitation may cease. It may be pushed forward until it shall become alike lawful in all the States, old as well as new, North as well as South. I have said, and I repeat, my wish is that the further spread of it may be arrested, and that it may be placed where the public mind shall rest in the belief that it is in the course of ultimate extinction. I have expressed that as my wish. . .

I confess, when I propose a certain measure of policy, it is not enough for me that I do not intend anything evil in the result, but it is incumbent on me to show that it has not a *tendency* to that result. I have met Judge Douglas in that point of view. I have not only made the declaration that I do not *mean* to produce a conflict between the States, but I have tried to show by fair reasoning, and I think I have shown to the minds of fair men, that I propose nothing but what has a most peaceful tendency. . . .

I have stated upon former occasions, and I may as well state again, what I understand to be the real issue in this controversy between Judge Douglas and myself. On the point of my wanting to make war between the free and the slave

States, there has been no issue between us. So, too, when he assumes that I am in favor of introducing a perfect social and political equality between the white and black races. These are false issues, upon which Judge Douglas has tried to force the controversy. There is no foundation in truth for the charge that I maintain either of these propositions. The real issue in this controversy — the one pressing upon every mind — is the sentiment on the part of one class that looks upon the institution of slavery *as a wrong*, and of another class that *does not* look upon it as a wrong. The sentiment that contemplates the institution of slavery in this country as a wrong is the sentiment of the Republican party. It is the sentiment around which all their actions — all their arguments circle — from which all their propositions radiate. They look upon it as being a moral, social and political wrong; and while they contemplate it as such, they nevertheless have due regard for its actual existence among us, and the difficulties of getting rid of it in any satisfactory way and to all the constitutional obligations thrown about it. Yet having a due regard for these, they desire a policy in regard to it that looks to its not creating any more danger. They insist that it should as far as may be, *be treated* as a wrong, and one of the methods of treating it as a wrong is to *make provision that it shall grow no larger*. They also desire a policy that looks to a peaceful end of slavery at some time, as being wrong. These are the views they entertain in regard to it as I understand them; and all their sentiments — all their arguments and propositions are brought within this range. I have said and I repeat it here, that if there be a man amongst us who does not think that the institution of slavery is wrong in any one of the aspects of which

I have spoken, he is misplaced and ought not to be with us. And if there be a man amongst us who is so impatient of it as a wrong as to disregard its actual presence among us and the difficulty of getting rid of it suddenly in a satisfactory way, and to disregard the constitutional obligations thrown about it, that man is misplaced if he is on our platform. We disclaim sympathy with him in practical action. He is not placed properly with us.

On this subject of treating it as a wrong, and limiting its spread, let me say a word. Has anything ever threatened the existence of this Union save and except this very institution of Slavery? What is it that we hold most dear amongst us? Our own liberty and prosperity. What has ever threatened our liberty and prosperity save and except this institution of Slavery? If this is true, how do you propose to improve the condition of things by enlarging Slavery — by spreading it out and making it bigger? You may have a wen or a cancer upon your person and not be able to cut it out lest you bleed to death; but surely it is no way to cure it, to engraft it and spread it over your whole body. That is no proper way of treating what you regard a wrong. You see this peaceful way of dealing with it as a wrong — restricting the spread of it, and not allowing it to go into new countries where it has not already existed. That is the peaceful way, the old-fashioned way, the way in which the fathers themselves set us the example.

On the other hand, I have said there is a sentiment which treats it as *not* being wrong. That is the Democratic sentiment of this day. I do not mean to say that every man who stands within that range positively asserts that it is right. That class will include all who positively assert that it is right, and all who like assert that it is right, and all who like

Judge Douglas treat it as indifferent and do not say it is either right or wrong. These two classes of men fall within the general class of those who do not look upon it as a wrong. And if there be among you anybody who supposes that he as a Democrat, can consider himself "as much opposed to slavery as anybody," I would like to reason with him. You never treat it as a wrong. What other thing that you consider as a wrong, do you deal with as you deal with that? Perhaps you *say* it is wrong, *but your leader never does, and you quarrel with anybody who says it is wrong.* Although you pretend to say so yourself you can find no fit place to deal with it as a wrong. You must not say anything about it in the free States, *because it is not here.* You must not say anything about it in the slave States, *because it is there.* You must not say anything about it in the pulpit, because that is religion and has nothing to do with it. You must not say anything about it in politics, *because that will disturb the security of "my place."* There is no place to talk about [it] as being a wrong, although you say yourself it *is* a wrong. . . .

That is the real issue. That is the issue that will continue in this country when these poor tongues of Judge Douglas and myself shall be silent. It is the eternal struggle between these two principles — right and wrong — throughout the world. They are the two principles that have stood face to face from the beginning of time; and will ever continue to struggle. The one is the common right of humanity and the other the divine right of kings. It is the same principle in whatever shape it develops itself. It is the same spirit that says, "You work and toil and earn bread, and I'll eat it." No matter in what shape it comes, whether from the mouth of a king who seeks to bestride the people of his own nation and live by the fruit of their labor, or from one race of men as an apology for enslaving another race, it is the same tyrannical principle. I was glad to express my gratitude at Quincy, and I re-express it here to Judge Douglas — *that he looks to no end of the institution of slavery.* That will help the people to see where the struggle really is. It will here-after place with us all men who really do wish the wrong may have an end. And whenever we can get rid of the fog which obscures the real question — when we can get Judge Douglas and his friends to avow a policy looking to its perpetua-tion — we can get out from among them that class of men and bring them to the side of those who treat it as a wrong. Then there will soon be an end of it, and that end will be its "ultimate extinction." Whenever the issue can be distinctly made, and all extraneous matter thrown out so that men can fairly see the real difference between the parties, this con-troversy will soon be settled, and it will be done peaceably too. There will be no war, no violence. It will be placed again where the wisest and best men of the world, placed it. . . .

H. Ford Douglass: LINCOLN, SLAVERY, AND EQUAL RIGHTS

The debate over slavery in the North was a three-cornered one among proponents of Douglas' program of popular sovereignty, supporters of Lincoln's program of congressional exclusion of slavery from the territories, and advocates of the abolitionist program of equal treatment of Negroes throughout the United States. One of the active spokesmen for the abolitionist program was H. Ford Douglass, a free Negro from Lincoln's home state of Illinois. In this speech, delivered just before the election of 1860, Douglass voiced the abolitionist demand for a policy of equal treatment and expressed his dissatisfaction with the programs of Lincoln and Douglas.

WE have four parties in this country that have marshalled themselves on the highway of American politics, asking for the votes of the American people to place them in possession of the government. We have what is called the Union party, led by Mr. Bell, of Tennessee; we have what is called the Democratic party, led by Stephen A. Douglas, of Illinois; we have the party called the Seceders, or the Slave-Code Democrats, led by John C. Breckinridge, of Kentucky, and then we have the Republican party, led by Abraham Lincoln, of Illinois. All of these parties ask for your support, because they profess to represent some principle. So far as the principles of freedom and the hopes of the black men are concerned, all these parties are barren and unfruitful; neither of them seeks to lift the negro out of his fetters, and rescue this day from odium and disgrace.

Take Abraham Lincoln. I want to know if any man can tell me the difference between the anti-slavery of Abraham Lincoln, and the anti-slavery of the old Whig party, or the anti-slavery of Henry Clay? Why, there is no difference between them. Abraham Lincoln is simply a Henry Clay Whig, and he believes just as Henry Clay believed in regard to this question. And Henry Clay was just as odious to the anti-slavery cause and anti-slavery men as ever was John C. Calhoun. In fact, he did as much to perpetuate negro slavery in this country as any other man who has ever lived. Henry Clay once said, "That is property which the law declares to be property," and that "two hundred years of legislation have sanctioned and sanctified property in slaves"! Wherever Henry Clay is today in the universe of God, that atheistic lie is with him, with all its tormenting memories.

I know Abraham Lincoln, and I know something about his anti-slavery. I know the Republicans do not like this kind of talk, because, while they are willing to steal our thunder, they are unwilling to submit to the conditions imposed upon

From *The Liberator*, vol. XXX, no. 28, July 13, 1860, pp. 109–110.

that party that assumes to be anti-slavery. They say that they cannot go as fast as you anti-slavery men go in this matter; that they cannot afford to be uncompromisingly honest, nor so radical as you Garrisonians; that they want to take time; that they want to do the work gradually. They say, "We must not be in too great a hurry to overthrow slavery; at least, we must take half a loaf, if we cannot get the whole." Now, my friends, I believe that the very best way to overthrow slavery in this country is to occupy the highest possible anti-slavery ground. Washington Irving tells a story of a Dutchman, who wanted to jump over a ditch, and he went back three miles in order to get a good start, and when he got up to the ditch, he had to sit down on the wrong side to get his breath. So it is with these political parties; they are compelled, they say, when they get up to the ditch of slavery, to stop and take breath.

I do not believe in the anti-slavery of Abraham Lincoln, because he is on the side of this Slave Power of which I am speaking, that has possession of the Federal Government. What does he propose to do? Simply to let the people and the Territories regulate their domestic institutions in their own way. In this great debate between Lincoln and Douglas in Illinois, when he was interrogated as to whether he was in favor of the admission of more slave States into the Union, he said, that so long as we owned the territories, he did not see any other way of doing than to admit those States when they made application, *with or without slavery*. Now, that is Douglas's doctrine; it is stealing the thunder of Stephen A. Douglas.

In regard to the repeal of the Fugitive Slave Law, Abraham Lincoln occupies the same position that the old Whig party occupied in 1852. They asserted then, in their platform, that they were not in favor of the repeal of that law, and they would do nothing to lessen its efficiency. What did he say at Freeport? Why, that the South was entitled to a Fugitive Slave Law; and although he thought the law could be modified a little, yet, he said, if he was in Congress, he would have it done in such a way as *not to lessen its efficiency!* Here, then, is Abraham Lincoln in favor of carrying out that infamous Fugitive Slave Law, that not only strikes down the liberty of every black man in the United States, but virtually the liberty of every white man as well; for, under that law, there is not a man in this presence who might not be arrested to-day upon the simple testimony of one man, and, after an *ex parte* trial, hurried off to slavery and to chains. *Habeas corpus,* trial by jury, — those great bulwarks of freedom, reared by the blood and unspeakable woe of your English ancestors, amidst the conflicts of a thousand years, — are struck down by this law; and the man whose name is inscribed upon the Presidential banner of the Republican party is in favor of keeping it upon the statute-book!

Not only would I arraign Mr. Lincoln, in regard to that law, for his pro-slavery character and principles, but when he was a member of the House of Representatives, in 1849, on the 10th day of January, he went through the District of Columbia, and consulted the prominent pro-slavery men and slaveholders of the District, and then went into the House of Representatives, and introduced, on his own responsibility, a fugitive slave law for the District of Columbia. It is well known that the law of 1793 did not apply to the District, and it was necessary, in order that slaveholders might catch their slaves who sought safety under the shadow of the capital, that a special law should be passed for the District of Columbia; and so Mr. Lincoln went down deeper into the pro-slavery pool than even Mr. Mason of Virginia did in the Fugitive Slave Law of 1850. Here, then, is the man who asks for your votes, and for the votes of the anti-slavery people of New England, who, on his own responsibility, without any temptation whatever, introduced into the District of Columbia a fugitive slave law. That is a fact for the consideration of anti-slavery men.

Then, there is another item which I want to bring out in this connection. I am a colored man; I am an American citizen; and I think that I am entitled to exercise the elective franchise. I am about twenty-eight years old, and I would like to vote very much. I think I am old enough to vote, and I think that, if I had a vote to give, I should know enough to place it on the side of freedom. No party, it seems to me, is entitled to the sympathy of anti-slavery men, unless that party is willing to extend to the black man all the rights of a citizen. I care nothing about that anti-slavery which wants to make the Territories free, while it is unwilling to extend to me, as a man, in the free States, all the rights of a man. In the State of Illinois, where I live — my adopted State — I have been laboring to make it a place fit for a decent man to live in. In that State, we have a code of black laws that would disgrace any Barbary State, or any uncivilized people in the far-off islands of the sea. Men of my complexion are not allowed to testify in a court of justice, where a white man is a party. If a white man happens to owe me anything, unless I can prove it by the testimony of a white man, I cannot collect the debt. Now, two years ago, I went through the State of Illinois for the purpose of getting signers to a petition, asking the Legislature to repeal the 'Testimony Law,' so as to permit colored men to testify against white men. I went to prominent Republicans, and among others, to Abraham Lincoln and Lyman Trumbull, and neither of them dared to sign that petition, to give me the right to testify in a court of justice! In the State of Illinois, they tax the colored people for every conceivable purpose. They tax the negro's property to support schools for the education of the white man's children, but the colored people are not permitted to enjoy any of the benefits resulting from that taxation. We are compelled to impose upon ourselves additional taxes, in order to educate our children. The State lays its iron hand upon the negro, holds him down, and puts the other hand into his pocket and steals his hard earnings, to educate the children of white men: and if we sent our children to school, Abraham Lincoln would kick them out, in the name of Republicanism and anti-slavery!

I have, then, something to say against the anti-slavery character of the Republican party. Not only are the Republicans of Illinois on the side of slavery, and against the rights of the negro, but even some of the prominent Republicans of Massachusetts are not acceptable anti-slavery men in that regard. In the Senate of the United States, some of your Senators make concessions to the Slave Power, by saying that they are not in favor of bringing about negro equality, just as Abraham Lincoln did down in Ohio two years ago. When he went there to stump that state, the colored people were agitating the question of suffrage in that State. The *Ohio Statesman*, a paper published in Columbus, asserted, on the morning of the day that Mr.

Lincoln made his speech, that he was in favor of negro equality; and Mr. Lincoln took pains at that time to deny the allegation, by saying that he was not in favor of bringing about the equality of the negro race; that he did not believe in making them voters, in placing them in the jury-box, or in ever bringing about the political equality of the races. He said that so long as they lived here, there must be an inferior and superior position, and that he was, as much as anybody else, in favor of assigning to white men the superior position. . . .

Hypocrisy is not a growth peculiar to American soil, but it has reached its most hateful development here. . . . God has given us a goodly land in which to build up an empire of thought; it ought also to be an empire of freedom. . . .

Abraham Lincoln: FIRST INAUGURAL ADDRESS

Lincoln assumed the role of architect of government policy even be-fore his inauguration as President. When the seven states of the lower South initiated secession proceedings after the election of 1860, Lincoln used his influence to persuade the leaders of the Republican party in Congress to hold firm to the principle of exclusion of slavery from the territories and to avoid any act which would imply recognition of the right of secession. Lincoln used the occasion of his inauguration on March 4, 1861, to explain the basis of his program and to inform the nation of the general principles which were to guide him in dealing with future developments in the secession crisis.

FELLOW citizens of the United States:

In compliance with a custom as old as the government itself, I appear before you to address you briefly, and to take, in your presence, the oath prescribed by the Constitution of the United States, to be taken by the President "before he enters on the execution of his office."

I do not consider it necessary, at present, for me to discuss those matters of administration about which there is no special anxiety, or excitement.

Apprehension seems to exist among the people of the Southern States, that by the accession of a Republican Administration, their property, and their peace, and personal security, are to be endangered. There has never been any reasonable cause for such apprehension. Indeed, the most ample evidence to the contrary has all the while existed, and been open to their inspection. It is found in nearly all the published speeches of him who now addresses you. I do but quote from one of those speeches when I declare that "I have no purpose, di-rectly or indirectly, to interfere with the institution of slavery in the States where it exists. I believe I have no lawful right to do so, and I have no inclination to do so.". . .

It is seventy-two years since the first inauguration of a President under our national Constitution. During that period fifteen different and greatly distinguished citizens, have, in succession, administered the executive branch of the government. They have conducted it through many perils; and, generally, with great success. Yet, with all this scope for precedent, I now enter upon the same task for the brief constitutional term of four years, under great and peculiar difficulty. A disruption of the Federal Union heretofore only menaced, is now formidably attempted.

I hold, that in contemplation of universal law, and of the Constitution, the Union of these States is perpetual. Perpetuity is implied, if not expressed, in the fundamental law of all national governments. It is safe to assert that no government proper, ever had a provision

Reprinted by permission from Roy P. Basler, ed., *The Collected Works of Abraham Lincoln* (New Brunswick, N. J.: Rutgers University Press, 1953), IV, 262–266, 268–271.

in its organic law for its own termination. Continue to execute all the express provisions of our national Constitution, and the Union will endure forever — it being impossible to destroy it, except by some action not provided for in the instrument itself.

Again, if the United States be not a government proper, but an association of States in the nature of contract merely, can it, as a contract, be peaceably unmade, by less than all the parties who made it? One party to a contract may violate it — break it, so to speak; but does it not require all to lawfully rescind it?

Descending from these general principles, we find the proposition that, in legal contemplation, the Union is perpetual, confirmed by the history of the Union itself. The Union is much older than the Constitution. It was formed, in fact, by the Articles of Association in 1774. It was matured and continued by the Declaration of Independence in 1776. It was further matured and the faith of all the then thirteen States expressly plighted and engaged that it should be perpetual, by the Articles of Confederation in 1778. And finally, in 1787, one of the declared objects for ordaining and establishing the Constitution, was *"to form a more perfect union."*

But if destruction of the Union, by one, or by a part only, of the States, be lawfully possible, the Union is *less* perfect than before the Constitution, having lost the vital element of perpetuity.

It follows from these views that no State, upon its own mere motion, can lawfully get out of the Union, — that *resolves* and *ordinances* to that effect are legally void; and that acts of violence, within any State or States, against the authority of the United States, are insurrectionary or revolutionary, according to circumstances.

I therefore consider that, in view of the Constitution and the laws, the Union is unbroken; and, to the extent of my ability, I shall take care, as the Constitution itself expressly enjoins upon me, that the laws of the Union be faithfully executed in all the States. Doing this I deem to be only a simple duty on my part; and I shall perform it, so far as practicable, unless my rightful masters, the American people, shall withhold the requisite means, or, in some authoritative manner, direct the contrary. I trust this will not be regarded as a menace, but only as the declared purpose of the Union that it *will* constitutionally defend, and maintain itself.

In doing this there needs to be no bloodshed or violence; and there shall be none, unless it be forced upon the national authority. The power confided to me, will be used to hold, occupy, and possess the property, and places belonging to the government, and to collect the duties and imposts; but beyond what may be necessary for these objects, there will be no invasion — no using of force against, or among the people anywhere. Where hostility to the United States, in any interior locality, shall be so great and so universal, as to prevent competent resident citizens from holding the Federal offices, there will be no attempt to force obnoxious strangers among the people for that object. While the strict legal right may exist in the government to enforce the exercises of these offices, the attempt to do so would be so irritating, and so nearly impracticable with all, that I deem it better to forego, for the time, the uses of such offices.

The mails, unless repelled, will continue to be furnished in all parts of the Union. So far as possible, the people everywhere shall have that sense of perfect security which is most favorable to calm thought and reflection. The course here indicated will be followed, unless current events, and experience, shall show a modification, or change, to be proper; and in every case and exigency, my best discretion will be exercised, according to circumstances actually existing, and with a view and a hope of a peaceful solution of the national troubles, and the restoration of fraternal sympathies and affections. . . .

Plainly, the central idea of secession, is the essence of anarchy. A majority, held in restraint by constitutional checks, and limitations, and always changing easily, with deliberate changes of popular opinions and sentiments, is the only true sovereign of a free people. Whoever rejects it, does, of necessity, fly to anarchy or to despotism. Unanimity is impossible; the rule of a minority, as a permanent arrangement, is wholly inadmissible; so that, rejecting the majority principle, anarchy, or despotism in some form, is all that is left . . . .

Physically speaking, we cannot separate. We cannot remove our respective sections from each other, nor build an impassable wall between them. A husband and wife may be divorced, and go out of the presence, and beyond the reach of each other; but the different parts of our country cannot do this. They cannot but remain face to face; and intercourse, either amicable or hostile, must continue between them. Is it possible then to make that intercourse more advantageous, or more satisfactory, *after* separation than *before?* Can aliens make treaties easier than friends can make laws? Can treaties be more faithfully enforced between aliens, than laws can among friends? Suppose you go to war, you cannot fight always; and when, after much loss on both sides, and no gain on either, you cease fighting, the identical old questions, as to terms of intercourse, are again upon you. . . .

The Chief Magistrate derives all his authority from the people, and they have conferred none upon him to fix terms for the separation of the States. The people themselves can do this also if they choose; but the executive, as such, has nothing to do with it. His duty is to administer the present government, as it came to his hands, and to transmit it, unimpaired by him, to his successor. . . .

In *your* hands, my dissatisfied fellow countrymen, and not in *mine,* is the momentous issue of civil war. The government will not assail *you.* *You* have no oath registered in Heaven to destroy the government, while *I* shall have the most solemn one to "preserve, protect and defend" it.

I am loth to close. We are not enemies, but friends. We must not be enemies. Though passion may have strained, it must not break our bonds of affection. The mystic chords of memory, stretching from every battle-field, and patriot grave, to every living heart and hearthstone, all over this broad land, will yet swell the chorus of the Union, when again touched, as surely they will be, by the better angels of our nature.

Stephen A. Douglas: A PLEA FOR PEACE AND UNION

The period following Lincoln's election to the Presidency was a bitter one for Stephen A. Douglas. His personal disappointment at losing the election was heightened by the feeling that the nation was being led to disaster by unwise policies. Recognizing that the seat of power lay in the Presidency, Douglas made a last effort to gain Lincoln's support for his program. In a series of speeches delivered in the Senate, Douglas urged Lincoln to modify his program by offering Southern leaders a compromise solution to the territorial question.

*A*RE *we prepared for war?* I do not mean that kind of preparation which consists of armies and navies, and supplies, and munitions of war, but are we prepared IN OUR HEARTS for war with our own brethren and kindred? I confess I am not. While I affirm that the Constitution is, and was intended to be, a bond of perpetual Union; while I can do no act and utter no word that will acknowledge or countenance the right of secession; while I affirm the right and duty of the Federal Government to use all legitimate means to enforce the laws, put down rebellion, and suppress insurrection, I will not meditate war, nor tolerate the idea, until every effort at peaceful adjustment shall have been exhausted, and the last ray of hope shall have deserted the patriot's heart. Then, and not till then, will I consider and determine what course my duty to my country may require me to pursue in such an emergency. In my opinion, war is disunion, certain, inevitable, irrevocable. I am for peace to save the Union. . . .

In my opinion, we have reached a point where disunion is inevitable, unless some compromise, founded upon mutual concession, can be made. I prefer compromise to war. I prefer concession to a dissolution of the Union. When I avow myself in favor of compromise, I do not mean that one side should give up all that it has claimed, nor that the other side should give up everything for which it has contended. Nor do I ask any man to come to my standard; but I simply say that I will meet every one half way who is willing to preserve the peace of the country, and save the Union from disruption upon principles of compromise and concession. . . .

There are several modes in which this irritating question may be withdrawn from Congress, peace restored, the rights of the States maintained, and the Union rendered secure. One of them — one to which I can cordially assent — has been presented by the venerable Senator from Kentucky, [Mr. Crittenden]. The journal of the committee of thirteen shows that I voted for it in committee. I am prepared to vote for it again. I shall not

From Douglas' speeches in Congress of Jan. 3, 1861, Jan. 31, 1861, and March 15, 1861, *Congressional Globe,* 36 Cong., 2nd Sess., pt. 1, p. 661; pt. 2, pp. 1459–1461; appendix, pp. 39, 41, 42.

occupy time now in discussing the question whether my vote to make a partition between the two sections, instead of referring the question to the people, will be consistent with my previous record or not. The country has no very great interest in my consistency. The preservation of this Union, the integrity of this Republic, is of more importance than party platforms or individual records. Hence I have no hesitation in saying to Senators on all sides of this Chamber, that I am prepared to act on this question with reference to the present exigencies of the case, as if I had never given a vote, or uttered a word, or had an opinion upon the subject.

Why cannot you Republicans accede to the reëstablishment and extension of the Missouri compromise line? You have sung peans enough in its praise, and uttered imprecations and curses enough on my head for its repeal, one would think, to justify you now in claiming a triumph by its reëstablishment. If you are willing to give up your party feelings — to sink the partisan in the patriot — and help me to reëstablish and extend that line, as a perpetual bond of peace between the North and the South, I will promise you never to remind you in the future of your denunciations of the Missouri compromise so long as I was supporting it, and of your praises of the same measure when we removed it from the statutebook, after you had caused it to be abandoned, by rendering it impossible for us to carry it out. I seek no partisan advantage; I desire no personal triumph. I am willing to let by-gones be by-gones with every man who, in this exigency, will show by his vote that he loves his country more than his party.

I presented to the committee of thirteen, and also introduced into the Senate, another plan by which the slavery question may be taken out of Congress and the peace of the country maintained. It is, that Congress shall make no law on the subject of slavery in the Territories, and that the existing *status* of each Territory on that subject, as it now stands by law, shall remain unchanged until it has fifty thousand inhabitants, when it shall have the right of self-government as to its domestic policy. . . .

. . . I believe this to be a fair basis of amicable adjustment. If you of the Republican side are not willing to accept this, nor the proposition of the Senator from Kentucky, [Mr. Crittenden,] pray tell us what you are willing to do? I address the inquiry to the Republicans alone, for the reason that in the committee of thirteen, a few days ago, every member from the South, including those from the cotton States, [Messrs. Toombs and Davis,] expressed their readiness to accept the proposition of my venerable friend from Kentucky [Mr. Crittenden] as a final settlement of the controversy, if tendered and sustained by the Republican members. Hence, the sole responsibility of our disagreement, and the only difficulty in the way of an amicable adjustment, is with the Republican party.

*   *   *

Now, sir, why should we not settle this question? The Senator from New York has shown us that the contest has gone on for twelve years; he has assumed that during those twelve years the South have had control of the Government, and given every possible protection to slavery in the Territories; and yet they have only succeeded in planting twenty-four slaves in all the Territories — Territories twenty-four times as large as the State of New York. Do not these facts show the utter fallacy of . . . attempting to plant slavery where the climate is adverse and the people do not want it; and the utter folly of the other side of . . . bringing this country to the very verge of disunion in order to prohibit slavery where the power of the Government could not make it exist?

This statement of facts shows conclusively that there is nothing practical in the question; that the demand for prohibition is unnecessary for the purposes for which it is set forth; that the demand for protection by this Government is utterly unavailing, even when you have the power in your own hands to carry it to the extreme. Why break up the Union upon an abstraction that has no practical results in it? Why cannot the one side give up its demand for prohibition, and the other for protection, and adopt an amendment to the Constitution in these words: "Congress shall have no power to legislate upon the subject of domestic servants anywhere, except to perform its duties under the Constitution in respect to fugitives from service, and the prohibition of the African slave trade?" Do that, and you will have peace; do that, and the Union will last forever; do that, and you do not extend slavery one inch, nor circumscribe it one inch; you do not emancipate a slave, and do not enslave a freeman. The practical result will be the same, so far as the slavery question is concerned, and this Union will last forever.

* * *

In my opinion, we have now reached a point where this agitation must close, and all the matters in controversy be finally determined by constitutional amendments, or civil war and the disruption of the Union are inevitable. . . .

I regret the determination, to which I apprehend the Republican Senators have come, to make no adjustment, entertain no proposition, and listen to no compromise of the matters in controversy.

I fear, from all the indications, that they are disposed to treat the matter as a party question, to be determined in caucus with reference to its effects upon the prospects of their party, rather than upon the peace of the country and the safety of the Union. I invoke their deliberate judgment whether it is not a dangerous experiment for any political party to demonstrate to the American people that the unity of their party is dearer to them than the Union of these States. The argument is, that the Chicago platform having been ratified by the people in a majority of the States must be maintained at all hazards, no matter what the consequences to the country. I insist that they are mistaken in the fact when they assert that this question was decided by the American people in the late election. The American people have not decided that they preferred the disruption of this Government, and civil war with all its horrors and miseries, to surrendering one iota of the Chicago platform. If you believe that the people are with you on this issue, let the question be submitted to the people on the proposition offered by the Senator from Kentucky, or mine, or any other fair compromise, and I will venture the prediction that your own people will ratify the proposed amendments to the Constitution, in order to take this slavery agitation out of Congress, and restore peace to the country, and insure the perpetuity of the Union.

Why not give the people a chance? It is an important crisis. There is now a different issue presented from that in the presidential election. I have no doubt that the people of Massachusetts, by an overwhelming majority, are in favor of a prohibition of slavery in the Territories by an act of Congress. An overwhelming majority of the same people were in favor of the instant prohibition of the African slave trade, on moral and religious grounds, when the Constitution was made. When they found that the Constitution could not be adopted and the Union preserved, without surrendering their objections on the slavery question, they, in the spirit of patriotism and of Christian feeling, preferred the lesser evil to the greater, and ratified the Constitution without their favorite provision in regard to slavery. Give them a chance to decide now between the ratification of these proposed amendments to the Constitution and the consequences which your policy will inevitably produce.

Why not allow the people to pass on these questions? All we have to do is to submit them to the States. If the people reject them, theirs will be the responsibility, and no harm will have been done by the reference. If they accept them, the country will be safe, and at peace. The political party which shall refuse to allow the people to determine for themselves at the ballot-box the issue between revolution and war on the one side, and obstinate adherence to a party platform on the other, will assume a fearful responsibility. A war upon a political issue, waged by the people of eighteen States against the people and domestic institutions of fifteen sister States, is a fearful and revolting thought. The South will be a unit, and desperate, under the belief that your object in waging war is their destruction, and not the preservation of the Union; that you meditate servile insurrection, and the abolition of slavery in the southern States, by fire and sword, in the name and under pretext of enforcing the laws and vindicating the authority of the Government. You know that such is the prevailing, and, I may say, unanimous opinion at the South;

and that ten million people are preparing for the terrible conflict under that conviction. . . .

It matters not, so far as the peace of the country and the preservation of the Union are concerned, whether the apprehensions of the southern people are well founded or not, so long as they believe them, and are determined to act upon that belief. If war comes, it must have an end at some time; and that termination, I apprehend, will be a final separation. Whether the war last one year, seven years, or thirty years, the result must be the same — a cessation of hostilities when the parties become exhausted, and a treaty of peace recognizing the separate independence of each section. The history of the world does not furnish an instance, where war has raged for a series of years between two classes of States, divided by a geographical line under the same national Government, which has ended in reconciliation and reunion. Extermination, subjugation, or separation, one of the three, must be the result of war between the northern and southern States. Surely, you do not expect to exterminate or subjugate ten million people, the entire population of one section, as a means of preserving amicable relations between the two sections!

I repeat, then, my solemn conviction, that war means disunion — final, irrevocable, eternal separation. I see no alternative, therefore, but a fair compromise, founded on the basis of mutual concessions, alike honorable, just, and beneficial to all parties, or civil war and disunion. Is there anything humiliating in a fair compromise of conflicting interests, opinions, and theories, for the sake of peace, union, and safety? Read the debates of the Federal convention, which formed our glorious Constitution, and you will find noble examples, worthy of imitation; instances where sages and patriots were willing to surrender cherished theories and principles of government, believed to be essential to the best form of society, for the sake of peace and unity.

I never understood that wise and good men ever regarded mutual concessions by such men as Washington, Madison, Franklin, and Hamilton, as evidences of weakness, cowardice, or want of patriotism. On the contrary, this spirit of conciliation and compromise has ever been considered, and will in all time be regarded as the highest evidence which their great deeds and immortal services ever furnished of their patriotism, wisdom, foresight, and devotion to their country and their race. Can we not afford to imitate their example in this momentous crisis? Are we to be told that we must not do our duty to our country lest we injure the party; that no compromise can be effected without violating the party platform upon which we were elected? Better that all party platforms be scattered to the winds; better that all political organizations be broken up; better that every public man and politician in America be consigned to political martyrdom, than that the Union be destroyed and the country plunged into civil war.

It seems that party platforms, pride of opinion, personal consistency, fear of political martyrdom, are the only obstacles to a satisfactory adjustment. Have we nothing else to live for but political position? Have we no other inducement, no other incentive to our efforts, our toils, and our sacrifices? Most of us have children, the objects of our tenderest affections and deepest solicitude, whom we hope to leave behind us to enjoy the rewards of our labors in a happy, prosperous, and united country, under the

best Government the wisdom of man ever devised or the sun of heaven ever shone upon. Can we make no concessions, no sacrifices, for the sake of our children, that they may have a country to live in, and a Government to protect them, when party platforms and political honors shall avail us nothing in the day of final reckoning?

*   *   *

. . . I desire to know from the Administration whether they mean peace or war; whether they mean to ask for military force adequate not only to hold the forts they have got, but to recapture those that have been lost, and to reduce to subjection and obedience all the people of all the States who have claimed, or shall claim, the right to secede; for it is folly to talk about the forts, unless we are going to do the other thing. It is morally wrong to collect revenue from a people that you do not protect. If you compel people to yield obedience to your laws, you must give them the protection of the laws. Hence the simple question is, whether, by military power, by the Army, the Navy, and the militia, we are going to subjugate those seceded States and hold them by military force in obedience to our laws until they so far change their inclinations as to obey them voluntarily? If this be the policy, I desire to know, and the country will demand to know, how large an army it will take. . . .

I repeat, it is time that the line of policy was adopted, and that the country knew it. In my opinion, we must choose, and that promptly, between one of three lines of policy:

1. The RESTORATION AND PRESERVATION OF THE UNION by such amendments to the Constitution as will insure the domestic tranquillity, safety,

and equality of all the States, and thus restore peace, unity, and fraternity, to the whole country.

2. A PEACEFUL DISSOLUTION of the Union, by recognizing the independence of such States as refuse to remain in the Union without such constitutional amendments, and the establishment of a liberal system of commercial and social intercourse with them by treaties of commerce and amity.

3. WAR, with a view to the subjugation and military occupation of those States which have seceded or may secede from the Union.

I repeat that, in my opinion, you must adopt and pursue one of these three lines of policy. The sooner you choose between them and proclaim your choice to the country, the better for you, the better for us, the better for every friend of liberty and constitutional government throughout the world. In my opinion, the first proposition is the best, and the last the worst. . . .

. . . I prefer . . . an amicable settlement to peaceable disunion; and I prefer it a thousand times to civil war. If we can adopt such amendments as will be satisfactory to Virginia, North Carolina, Tennessee, and the border States, the same plan of pacification which will satisfy them will create a Union party in the cotton States which will soon embrace a large majority of the people in those States, and bring them back of their own free will and accord; and thus restore, strengthen, and perpetuate the glorious old Union forever. I repeat, whatever guarantees will satisfy Maryland and the border States [the States now in the Union] will create a Union party in the seceded States that will bring them back by the voluntary action of their own people. You can restore and preserve the Union in that mode. You

can do it in no other. . . .

But we are told, and we hear it repeated everywhere, that we must find out whether we have got a Government. "Have we a Government?" is the question; and we are told we must test that question by using the military power to put down all discontented spirits. Sir, this question, "have we a Government?" has been propounded by every tyrant who has tried to keep his feet on the necks of the people since the world began. When the Barons demanded *Magna Charta* from King John at Runnymede, he exclaimed, "have we a government?" and called for his army to put down the discontented barons. When Charles I attempted to collect the ship money in violation of the constitution of England, and in disregard of the rights of the people, and was resisted by them, he exclaimed, "have we a government? We cannot treat with rebels; put down the traitors; we must show that we have a government." When James II was driven from the throne of England for trampling on the liberties of the people, he called for his army, and exclaimed, "let us show that we have a government!" When George III called upon his army to put down the rebellion in America, Lord North cried lustily, "no compromise with traitors; let us demonstrate that we have a government." When, in 1848, the people rose upon their tyrants all over Europe and demanded guarantees for their rights, every crowned head exclaimed, "have we a government?" and appealed to the army to vindicate their authority and to enforce the law.

Sir, the history of the world does not fail to condemn the folly, weakness, and wickedness of that Government which drew its sword upon its own people when they demanded guarantees for their rights. This cry, that we must have a Government, is merely following the example of the besotted Bourbon, who never learned anything by misfortune, never forgave an injury, never forgot an affront. Must we demonstrate that we have got a Government, and coerce obedience without reference to the justice or injustice of the complaints? Sir, whenever ten million people proclaim to you, with one unanimous voice, that they apprehend their rights, their firesides, and their family altars are in danger, it becomes a wise Government to listen to the appeal, and to remove the apprehension. History does not record an example where any human government has been strong enough to crush ten million people into subjection when they believed their rights and liberties were imperiled, without first converting the government itself into a despotism, and destroying the last vestige of freedom. . . .

If we consider this question calmly, and make such amendments as will convince the people of the southern States that they are safe and secure in their persons, in their property, and in their family relations, within the Union, we can restore and preserve it. If we cannot satisfy the people of the border States that they may remain in the Union with safety, dissolution is inevitable. Then the simple question comes back, what shall be the policy of the Union men of this country? Shall it be peace, or shall it be war? The President of the United States holds the destiny of this country in his hands. I believe he means peace, and war will be averted, unless he is overruled by the disunion portion of his party. We all know the irrepressible conflict is going on in their camp; even debating whether Fort Sumter shall be surrendered when it is impossible to hold it; whether Major Anderson shall not be kept there until he starves to death, or applies the torch with his own hand to the match that blows him and his little garrison into eternity, for fear that somebody of the Republican party might say you had backed down. What man in all America, with a heart in his bosom, who knows the facts connected with Fort Sumter, can hesitate in saying that duty, honor, patriotism, humanity, require that Anderson and his gallant band should be instantly withdrawn? Sir, I am not afraid to say so. I would scorn to take a party advantage or manufacture partisan capital out of an act of patriotism.

Then, throw aside this petty squabble about how you are to get along with your pledges before election; meet the issues as they are presented; do what duty, honor, and patriotism require, and appeal to the people to sustain you. Peace is the only policy that can save the country or save your party. Let peace be proclaimed as the policy, and you will find that a thrill of joy will animate the heart of every patriot in the land; confidence will be restored; business will be revived; joy will gladden every heart; bonfires will blaze upon the hilltops and in the valleys, and the church bells will proclaim the glad tidings in every city, town, and village in America, and the applause of a grateful people will greet you everywhere. Proclaim the policy of war, and there will be gloom and sadness and despair pictured upon the face of every patriot in the land. A war of kindred, family, and friends; father against son, mother against daughter, brother against brother, to subjugate one half of this country into obedience to the other half; if you do not mean this, if you mean peace, let . . . the President . . . speak the word "peace"; and thirty million people will bless him with their prayers, and honor him with their shouts of joy.

Editorial Comment: LET THEM GO IN PEACE

The newspapers of the North kept up a continuing debate on public policy in the months following Lincoln's election. Some editors urged the adoption of Douglas' program of compromise on the territorial question; others supported Lincoln's policy of exclusion of slavery from the territories; and still others called for a comprehensive program to secure equal treatment for the Negro throughout the nation. As the secession crisis grew more serious, a fourth group came to the fore urging the President to "let the Southern States go in peace." Support for this position came from Republicans and Democrats, from those who felt that permanent separation was more desirable than war, and those who believed that if the Southern States were left alone, they would eventually sue for readmission to the union on terms favorable to the North. The following editorials present a sampling of these arguments.

Cincinnati Daily Press,
    November 21, 1860

The thing that politicians in their haste, are most likely to overlook in [is?] the organic principle of their own government, perhaps it might be said that this is the thing of which, in general, they have the least practical conception. We all admit that the organic principle of our form of polity is the right of self-government — the will of the people constantly active in the frame-work and administration. We hold that the right of self-government is a native right, inherent in humanity, and vested, for its own purposes, in every body of people; and yet we are prone to forget that, as a corollary from this idea, we have no title to impose any species of constraint upon the self-governing power of other communities. . . .

South Carolina — we employ the name of a single State to indicate the whole of those be they more or less, who assume a similar position — South Carolina *talks* of seceding from the Confederacy of North American States; and the question — urgent in proportion to the probability that she will carry her talk into effect — is, What then? . . .

We believe that the right of any member of this Confederacy to dissolve its political relations with the others and assume an independent position is *absolute* — that, in other words, if South Carolina wants to go out of the Union, she has the right to do so, and no party or power may justly say her nay. This we suppose to be the doctrine of the Declaration of Independence when it affirms that governments are instituted for the protection of men in their lives, liberties, and the pursuit of happiness; and that "Whenever any form of government becomes destructive of these ends, it is the right of the people to alter or abolish it, and to institute new government, laying its foundation on such principles, and organizing its powers in such form, as to them shall seem most likely to effect their safety and happiness."

Whether the Government of the

United States is such an one as is best calculated to protect the lives, liberties and so forth, of the people of South Carolina, is a question which they alone are legally qualified to decide. We may have our opinions; but our opinions, whatever they may be, are not, and cannot be made, binding upon them. When the people of the British Colonies declared the Government of the Mother Country intolerable, they did it as the result of their own reflection and experience; nor did they deem it necessary to inquire whether King George, his counsellors or his home subjects, concurred in their convictions. They thought it wrong and a burden, and therefore they threw it off. The world has pronounced a clear verdict in favor of their right to choose, and of the correctness of their conclusions.

If this view of the legal aspects of the case is correct, it goes to settle the entire question. What is to be done? Simply nothing. Will we go to imitate the conduct of the "British tyrant," which we have in so many thousand forms condemned, and send armies and navies to South Carolina to reduce her to subjection? The idea of forcing men to belong to and carry on their share of the machinery of a government — of which the very essence is the free will of the constituent parts to act as they please, or not to act if they prefer, is to the last degree preposterous. Let South Carolina, in God's name, go if she wants to. The fact that she does want to, constitutes all the title that is necessary. Let her go in peace; and the States of the North would be violators of the fundamental doctrine of the Declaration of American Independence, if they should take any forcible measures to prevent her departure. . . .

Indianapolis Daily Journal,
 December 22, 1860

South Carolina has seceded. The mysterious operation was performed on Thursday at half past one post meridian. It appears to have been done "as easy as rolling off a log." If anybody has an idea of the facility implied in that phrase he can judge how easily South Carolina broke the Union. It may not be unworthy of remark that the sun rose on Friday morning very much as usual, and, either in joy or curiosity, made a decided effort to get through the clouds far enough to see the hole Carolina had left. The world moved on with no perceptible indication that it felt the "rent" the "envious" State had made in its integrity. Somebody announced it in Congress, and somebody cheered over it in Charleston, and secession was accomplished, and its terrors fairly encountered. Well, we are a severed nation. We are a divided house. And we are none the worse for it. All the mischief that the apprehension of disunion could do has been done, and disunion itself can do nothing if we do not force it to. We are well rid of South Carolina, if we are only wise enough to count it a riddance, and nothing worse. She can do far less harm out of the Union if we let her go out quietly, than she has always done in it, and can now do in double measure if she is forcibly kept in. We insist that she shall go out, and we shall thank God that we have had a good riddance of bad rubbish. South Carolina has always been a nuisance, only lacking the importance which an attempt at "coercion" would give her to be magnified into a pestilence, and we think we owe her so much gratitude for trying to leave us that we should help her on the way. If other States follow her, let them. If all the South follows her, let it. If they can't endure an association with us except on terms which ignore the vital principle of the original compact between us, and impose on *us* the support of slavery, we should be ashamed to ask them to stay. In God's name, and for humanity's sake, let them go in peace, live with their cherished institution while they can, prosper if it be Heaven's purpose, or within man's power, and if they ever learn that a great wrong can never be made the foundation of a great government, they may be willing, in the ruin of their hopes, to seek a refuge in the abandoned old Government, and abide there peacefully forever.

But this policy, the dictate of humanity and wisdom, as we conceive it to be, is not in favor with many warm Republicans. They insist . . . that it is the duty of the nation to preserve itself, and they quote Gen. Jackson and the Chicago Platform for the necessity of preserving the Union at all hazards. They argue, and nobody ever denied it, that secession is not permitted by the Constitution, and if one State may go out all may go, and then where will the nation be? True, but oh! sagacious patriots tell us where will the nation be if you attempt to keep it together by instituting a war between its members? — How will *that* process save the Union? "The Union shall be preserved," you say. So say we. But we insist that it shan't be ruined in the act of preservation. We don't believe in pickling a putrifaction [*sic*]. The Union *preserved* is worth any effort, except the surrender of its vital principle. But a civil war is not preservation. It is sure, speedy, overwhelming ruin. War, instead of preserving the Union, must rend it first, and ruin the fragments afterwards. Is any man so blind as not to see that? Is any man so devoted to the idea of "enforcing the laws" and "maintaining our glorious Constitution" as not to see

that maintaining it by civil war is the surest way to destroy it? The *right* to demand obedience of the seceding States to the Constitution they have adopted, and the laws they have themselves enacted, is indisputable. But if they can only be made to obey by fighting them the process is too expensive for the result. We can afford to do without their obedience, and without them, better than we can afford to ruin ourselves to retain either. Therefore, inconsistent as it may appear, while we hold that the Constitution requires the chastisement of rebellious States, we hold that humanity, our own interests, and the demands of this enlightened age, require us to stay our hands. There is a higher consideration than the Constitution, and it is the good which the Constitution was intended to effect. That instrument is only a means to secure an end, a law to preserve liberty, property and happiness to all under it. If its enforcement cannot secure those objects, then it is our *duty* to secure them without the Constitution. Now will any man say that a war between the North and South, to enforce the obedience of the latter to the Constitution, will preserve liberty, or property, or promote human happiness? We presume not. Every man can see that it is the most direct way to destroy all three. Freedom will not be more firmly established in the North by it, and if it be established in the South it can only be by a servile war promoted by the civil war, and *that* is a dear price to pay for emancipation anywhere. We eagerly proclaim now that we never would encourage it, and its character will not be changed, though our feelings may be, by a civil war. There is nothing to gain for liberty then by war. And it is an insult to common sense to prove that it cannot benefit property or personal happiness. War, therefore, would enforce the Constitution, which was intended to promote these great objects, at the expense of defeating the very objects it was intended to secure. A strong government is not worth so much as peace between brethren. If the Federal Government were as strong as the Russian autocracy it would be a poor compensation for the blood, and money, and opportunities for good, lost in making it so.

The world is going to climb to a higher philosophy of government than that which underlies monarchies and grew out of "the Divine right of kings." That philosophy claims the preservation of a government as its highest duty. The nobler philosophy demands that the objects of a government shall not be sacrificed to the government; that the end shall not be lost to save the means. — And if blood is to be spilled in maintaining one government over a people, when the people want another that they believe will benefit them as much, it is blood needlessly and cruelly spilled. The statesman can always see where to draw the line between the demand of a people for a change of government and the resistance of outlaws to wholesome restraints. Kossuth gave the world a higher and nobler idea of international law, in his plea for the aid of other nations to those struggling against oppression, than it ever had before, and the United States, by wisely applying the law avowed in her own Declaration of Independence, in the present crisis, may give the world a higher idea of the duties of governments than has yet been taught by man or nation.

This view of the duty of governments, which we are only confirmed in by each new examination, shows us the course to be pursued towards South Carolina. It is to let her go freely and entirely, let loose all revenue chains and postal cords, and push her out into a separate national existence, if not with good wishes at least without resistance. Henry Stanbery, the celebrated Ohio lawyer, in his speech at the Cincinnati Union meeting last Wednesday, contended that it was easy to coerce South Carolina without bloodshed, by simply blockading her ports. He opposed coercion if it involved war, but he was in favor of bloodless coercion. This is the position of a lawyer, not of a statesman. It is not a wise policy, but a quibble. We must do one of two things with South Carolina. We must either compel her obedience, or let her pass away from our control into her own. Mr. Stanbery's plan is to enforce the laws, without enforcing obedience, to collect the duties at Fort Moultrie, or out at sea, so as to keep the South Carolinians subject to our laws, and yet keep ourselves out of their reach. This is manifestly impossible. If South Carolina pretends to be an independent government, she *must* control her own ports, and if we blockade them she must drive us out. It is as absolutely necessary to her national existence as the air is to individual existence. By blockading their ports, therefore, we only resort to a trick to bring the first attack from South Carolina, instead of making it ourselves. — And that trick is unworthy of a great nation. If we are right we can begin the attack, without seeking pretexts. If we are not right, we are only showing cowardice as well as cruelty, in resorting to such a trick. There is, therefore, no escape from a war, if we refuse to admit the independence of South Carolina. — Mr. Stanbery does not avoid it. He only changes the first blow from one to the other. We must, then, determine either to fight openly and at once, or openly and freely permit South Carolina to depart. If we fight her, we shall fight every State in the South. — It is idle to blink this fact. Sooner or later, by sympathy, by relationship, by business connections, by volunteers from the States above leaving fathers, mothers, and brothers at home to grow more and more indifferent to the Union as their relatives are more and more bloodily mixed up with disunion, by a thousand influences, the border States will be drawn gradually into the fight, and before it is over the whole South will be fighting the whole North. This we regard as the inevitable result of a war with South Carolina. And a war, we believe, is a thousand times worse evil than the loss of a State, or a dozen States, that hate us, and will not stay with us without ruling us. We don't believe in standing on trifles or technical difficulties. Let us consider South Carolina a foreign nation the hour she gives the Federal Government notice of her secession, and in spite of all obstructions and questions of property, treat with her for an adjustment of our common debts and common property, and for the arrangement of treaties for the continuance of business. If we do so disunion will soon kill itself. If we attempt to kill it with bayonet and ball it will wound us fearfully before we can succeed, and when we have succeeded, its dead body will be as pestilent as its living body. We shall be burthened as badly to carry the corpse as to bear the restive and struggling live carcass.

Kenosha Wisconsin Democrat,
    January 11, 1861
    . . . No greater mistake can be made by any one, than to suppose a people accustomed to political free agency, can be chained together with an iron fatalism, in the bonds of an unwilling confederacy. The very freedom claimed by every indi-

vidual citizen, precludes the idea of compulsory association, as individuals, as communities, or as States. The very germ of liberty is the right of forming our own governments, enacting our own laws, and choosing our own political associates. The most valuable gift has lost its worth, if we are not free to reject it; and governmental protection is another name for tyrannical *surveillance* when forced on an unwilling people. The right of secession inheres to the people of every sovereign state. Governments were made by them, and can be unmade. Constitutions are adopted and repealed, by every free people. What any state by act or compact, has done; if it violate no vested right she may undo. The laws of one legislature, are repealable by the next with this single limitation. It has ever been the doctrine of the Democratic party that no generation can take from its successors by any act of legislation, the power to amend or repeal. This should be obvious to all. Without this right of each generation to pass on the question of its own rights and interests, there could be no progress in legislation, or in civilization. Deny this principle, and we are to-day the subjects of laws enacted a thousand years ago. The power to make laws, and establish governments, implies the power to unmake them; as the major proposition contains the minor. By this test the right of secession is maintained. South Carolina voted herself into the Union; she can vote herself out. *The Constitution of the United States was ratified by several of the states, with this express understanding.* This alone, would determine the right of secession. If eight of ten men agree to terms of partnership, and the other two state at the time of *their* agreement what they consider its terms and requirements are; if assented to by the others, this interpretation becomes a part of the compact. This right was ably vindicated by Mr. Nicholson of Virginia at the time of its ratification by that state. Many delegates were opposed to voting for the Constitution until all the other states had assented to this view of it. Mr. Nicholson contended this delay was unnecessary, for if Virginia adopted it on this condition, a refusal to recognize this interpretation would absolve her from all obligation to it. South Carolina took then precisely the same stand she does to-day for the rights of States. The celebrated Virginia and Kentucky resolutions do but embody the same principle.

The framers of the constitution hoped, and no doubt expected the Union to be perpetual; but they confessed it could only be perpetuated by the cheerful obedience of a willing people. They expected a time to come when one or more of the States should determine to secede. The[y] refused to incorporate a clause in the constitution enabling Congress or the President to use force against a seceding state. They declared any state had an inherent right to secede at pleasure, and a forcible union would be an invasion of that right. Mr. Madison expressly stated that he was opposed to the use of any force to unite the states, or to keep them united. He said any attempt to use force would involve the country in civil war, and forever separate the states. This accounts for the lack of constitutional prohibition of secession. . . .

Abraham Lincoln: MESSAGE TO CONGRESS, JULY 4, 1861

Lincoln's message to Congress of July 4, 1861 was submitted almost three months after the outbreak of war and contains an account of his stewardship in the period preceding the war. It stands as the President's only general discussion of his role in the events leading to the coming of the Civil War. Like many of Lincoln's state papers, it is both a perceptive analysis of the underlying issues of the crisis and a detailed brief for the policies he pursued. A reading of the message provides an insight into the process by which Lincoln made his crucial decisions as well as an understanding of the manner in which he defended them before Congress and the general public.

FELLOW-CITIZENS of the Senate and House of Representatives: . . .

At the beginning of the present Presidential term, four months ago, the functions of the Federal Government were found to be generally suspended within the several States of South Carolina, Georgia, Alabama, Mississippi, Louisiana, and Florida, excepting only those of the Post Office Department.

Within these States, all the Forts, Arsenals, Dock-yards, Customhouses, and the like, including the movable and stationary property in, and about them, had been seized, and were held in open hostility to this Government, excepting only Forts Pickens, Taylor, and Jefferson, on, and near the Florida coast, and Fort Sumter, in Charleston harbor, South Carolina. The Forts thus seized had been put in improved condition; new ones had been built; and armed forces had been organized, and were organizing, all avowedly with the same hostile purpose.

The Forts remaining in the possession of the Federal government, in, and near, these States, were either besieged or menaced by warlike preparations; and especially Fort Sumter was nearly surrounded by well-protected hostile batteries, with guns equal in quality to the best of its own, and outnumbering the latter as perhaps ten to one. A disproportionate share, of the Federal muskets and rifles, had somehow found their way into these States, and had been seized, to be used against the government. Accumulations of the public revenue, lying within them, had been seized for the same object. The Navy was scattered in distant seas; leaving but a very small part of it within the immediate reach of the government. Officers of the Federal Army and Navy, had resigned in great numbers; and, of those resigning, a large proportion had taken up arms against the government. Simultaneously, and in connection, with all this, the purpose to sever the Federal Union, was openly avowed. In accordance with this pur-

Reprinted by permission from Roy P. Basler, ed., *The Collected Works of Abraham Lincoln* (New Brunswick, N. J.: Rutgers University Press, 1953), IV, 421–426, 431–441.

pose, an ordinance had been adopted in each of these States, declaring the States, respectively, to be separated from the National Union. A formula for instituting a combined government of these states had been promulgated; and this illegal organization, in the character of confederate States was already invoking recognition, aid, and intervention, from Foreign Powers.

Finding this condition of things, and believing it to be an imperative duty upon the incoming Executive, to prevent, if possible, the consummation of such attempt to destroy the Federal Union, a choice of means to that end became indispensable. This choice was made; and was declared in the Inaugural address. The policy chosen looked to the exhaustion of all peaceful measures, before a resort to any stronger ones. It sought only to hold the public places and property, not already wrested from the Government, and to collect the revenue; relying for the rest, on time, discussion, and the ballot-box. It promised a continuance of the mails, at government expense, to the very people who were resisting the government; and it gave repeated pledges against any disturbance to any of the people, or any of their rights. Of all that which a president might constitutionally, and justifiably, do in such a case, everything was forborne, without which, it was believed possible to keep the government on foot.

On the 5th of March, (the present incumbent's first full day in office) a letter of Major Anderson, commanding at Fort Sumter, written on the 28th of February, and received at the War Department on the 4th of March, was, by that Department, placed in his hands. This letter expressed the professional opinion of the writer, that re-inforcements could not be thrown into that Fort within the time for

his relief, rendered necessary by the limited supply of provisions, and with a view of holding possession of the same, with a force of less than twenty thousand good, and well-disciplined men. This opinion was concurred in by all the officers of his command; and their *memoranda* on the subject, were made enclosures of Major Anderson's letter. The whole was immediately laid before Lieutenant General Scott, who at once concurred with Major Anderson in opinion. On reflection, however, he took full time, consulting with other officers, both of the Army and the Navy; and, at the end of four days, came reluctantly, but decidedly, to the same conclusions as before. He also stated at the same time that no such sufficient force was then at the control of the Government, or could be raised, and brought to the ground, within the time when the provisions in the Fort would be exhausted. In a purely military point of view, this reduced the duty of the administration, in the case, to the mere matter of getting the garrison safely out of the Fort.

It was believed, however, that to so abandon that position, under the circumstances, would be utterly ruinous; that the *necessity* under which it was to be done, would not be fully understood — that, by many, it would be construed as a part of a *voluntary* policy — that, at home, it would discourage the friends of the Union, embolden its adversaries, and go far to insure to the latter, a recognition abroad — that, in fact, it would be our national destruction consummated. This could not be allowed. Starvation was not yet upon the garrison; and ere it would be reached, *Fort Pickens* might be reinforced. This last, would be a clear indication of *policy*, and would better enable the country to accept the evacuation of Fort Sumter, as a military *necessity.* An order was at once directed to be sent for the landing of the troops from the Steamship Brooklyn, into Fort Pickens. This order could not go by land, but must take the longer, and slower route by sea. The first return news from the order was received just one week before the fall of Fort Sumter. The news itself was, that the officer commanding the Sabine, to which vessel the troops had been transferred from the Brooklyn, acting upon some *quasi* armistice of the late administration, (and of the existence of which, the present administration, up to the time the order was despatched, had only too vague and uncertain rumors, to fix attention) had refused to land the troops. To now re-inforce Fort Pickens, before a crisis would be reached at Fort Sumter was impossible — rendered so by the near exhaustion of provisions in the latter-named Fort. In precaution against such a conjuncture, the government had, a few days before, commenced preparing an expedition, as well adapted as might be, to relieve Fort Sumter, which expedition was intended to be ultimately used, or not, according to circumstances. The strongest anticipated case, for using it, was now presented; and it was resolved to send it forward. As had been intended, in this contingency, it was also resolved to notify the Governor of South Carolina, that he might expect an attempt would be made to provision the Fort; and that, if the attempt should not be resisted, there would be no effort to throw in men, arms, or ammunition, without further notice, or in case of an attack upon the Fort. This notice was accordingly given; whereupon the Fort was attacked, and bombarded to its fall, without even awaiting the arrival of the provisioning expedition.

It is thus seen that the assault upon, and reduction of, Fort Sumter, was, in no sense, a matter of self defence on the part of the assailants. They well knew that the garrison in the Fort could, by no possibility, commit aggression upon them. They knew — they were expressly notified — that the giving of bread to the few brave and hungry men of the garrison, was all which would on that occasion be attempted, unless themselves, by resisting so much, should provoke more. They knew that this Government desired to keep the garrison in the Fort, not to assail them, but merely to maintain visible possession, and thus to preserve the Union from actual, and immediate dissolution — trusting, as hereinbefore stated, to time, discussion, and the ballot-box, for final adjustment; and they assailed, and reduced the Fort, for precisely the reverse object — to drive out the visible authority of the Federal Union, and thus force it to immediate dissolution.

That this was their object, the Executive well understood; and having said to them in the inaugural address, "You can have no conflict without being yourselves the aggressors," he took pains, not only to keep this declaration good, but also to keep the case so free from the power of ingenious sophistry, as that the world should not be able to misunderstand it. By the affair at Fort Sumter, with its surrounding circumstances, that point was reached. Then, and thereby, the assailants of the Government, began the conflict of arms, without a gun in sight, or in expectancy, to return their fire, save only the few in the Fort, sent to that harbor, years before, for their own protection, and still ready to give that protection, in whatever was lawful. In this act, discarding all else, they have forced upon the country, the distinct issue: "Immediate dissolution, or blood."

And this issue embraces more than the fate of these United States. It presents to the whole family of man, the question, whether a constitutional republic, or a democracy — a government of the people, by the same people — can, or cannot, maintain its territorial integrity, against its own domestic foes. It presents the question, whether discontented individuals, too few in numbers to control administration, according to organic law, in any case, can always, upon the pretences made in this case, or on any other pretences, or arbitrarily, without any pretence, break up their Government, and thus practically put an end to free government upon the earth. It forces us to ask: "Is there, in all republics, this inherent, and fatal weakness?" "Must a government, of necessity, be too *strong* for the liberties of its own people, or too *weak* to maintain its own existence?"

So viewing the issue, no choice was left but to call out the war power of the Government; and so to resist force, employed for its destruction, by force, for its preservation. . . .

It is now recommended that you give the legal means for making this contest a short, and a decisive one; that you place at the control of the government, for the work, at least four hundred thousand men, and four hundred millions of dollars. That number of men is about one tenth of those of proper ages within the regions where, apparently, *all* are willing to engage; and the sum is less than a twentythird part of the money value owned by the men who seem ready to devote the whole. A debt of six hundred millions of dollars *now*, is a less sum per head, than was the debt of our revolution, when we came out of that struggle; and the money value in the country now, bears even a greater proportion of

what it was *then*, than does the population. Surely each man has as strong a motive *now*, to *preserve* our liberties, as each had *then*, to *establish* them.

A right result, at this time, will be worth more to the world, than ten times the men, and ten times the money. The evidence reaching us from the country, leaves no doubt, that the material for the work is abundant; and that it needs only the hand of legislation to give it legal sanction, and the hand of the Executive to give it practical shape and efficiency. One of the greatest perplexities of the government, is to avoid receiving troops faster than it can provide for them. In a word, the people will save their government, if the government itself, will do its part, only indifferently well.

It might seem, at first thought, to be of little difference whether the present movement at the South be called "secession" or "rebellion." The movers, however, well understand the difference. At the beginning, they knew they could never raise their treason to any respectable magnitude, by any name which implies *violation* of law. They knew their people possessed as much of moral sense, as much of devotion to law and order, and as much pride in, and reverence for, the history, and government, of their common country, as any other civilized, and patriotic people. They knew they could make no advancement directly in the teeth of these strong and noble sentiments. Accordingly they commenced by an insidious debauching of the public mind. They invented an ingenious sophism, which, if conceded, was followed by perfectly logical steps, through all the incidents, to the complete destruction of the Union. The sophism itself is, that any state of the Union may, *consistently* with the national Constitution, and therefore *lawfully,* and *peacefully,* withdraw from the Union, without the consent of the Union, or of any other state. The little disguise that the supposed right is to be exercised only for just cause, themselves to be the sole judge of its justice, is too thin to merit any notice.

With rebellion thus sugar-coated, they have been drugging the public mind of their section for more than thirty years; and, until at length, they have brought many good men to a willingness to take up arms against the government the day *after* some assemblage of men have enacted the farcical pretense of taking their State out of the Union, who could have been brought to no such thing the day *before.*

This sophism derives much — perhaps the whole — of its currency, from the assumption, that there is some omnipotent, and sacred supremacy, pertaining to a *State* — to each State of our Federal Union. Our States have neither more, nor less power, than that reserved to them, in the Union, by the Constitution — no one of them ever having been a State *out* of the Union. The original ones passed into the Union even *before* they cast off their British colonial dependence; and the new ones each came into the Union directly from a condition of dependence, excepting Texas. And even Texas, in its temporary independence, was never designated a State. The new ones only took the designation of States, on coming into the Union, while that name was first adopted for the old ones, in, and by, the Declaration of Independence. Therein the "United Colonies" were declared to be "Free and Independent States"; but, even then, the object plainly was not to declare their independence of *one another,* or of the Union; but directly the contrary, as their

mutual pledge, and their mutual action, before, at the time, and afterwards, abundantly show. The express plighting of faith, by each and all of the original thirteen, in the Articles of Confederation, two years later, that the Union shall be perpetual, is most conclusive. Having never been States, either in substance, or in name, *outside* of the Union, whence this magical omnipotence of "State rights," asserting a claim of power to lawfully destroy the Union itself? Much is said about the "sovereignty" of the States; but the word, even, is not in the national Constitution; nor, as is believed, in any of the State constitutions. What is a "sovereignty," in the political sense of the term? Would it be far wrong to define it "A political community, without a political superior"? Tested by this, no one of our States, except Texas, ever was a sovereignty. And even Texas gave up the character on coming into the Union; by which act, she acknowledged the Constitution of the United States, and the laws and treaties of the United States made in pursuance of the Constitution, to be, for her, the supreme law of the land. The States have their *status* in the Union, and they have no other *legal status.* If they break from this, they can only do so against law, and by revolution. The Union, and not themselves separately, procured their independence, and their liberty. By conquest, or purchase, the Union gave each of them, whatever of independence, and liberty, it has. The Union is older than any of the States; and, in fact, it created them as States. Originally, some dependent colonies made the Union; and, in turn, the Union threw off their old dependence, for them, and made them States, such as they are. Not one of them ever had a State constitution, independent of the Union. Of course, it is not forgotten that all the new States framed their constitutions, before they entered the Union; nevertheless, dependent upon, and preparatory to, coming into the Union.

Unquestionably the States have the powers, and rights, reserved to them in, and by the National Constitution; but among these, surely, are not included all conceivable powers, however, mischievous, or destructive; but, at most, such only, as were known in the world, at the time, as governmental powers; and certainly, a power to destroy the government itself, had never been known as a governmental — as a merely administrative power. This relative matter of National power, and State rights, as a principle, is no other than the principle of *generality,* and *locality.* Whatever concerns the whole, should be confided to the whole — to the general government; while, whatever concerns *only* the State, should be left exclusively, to the State. This is all there is of original principle about it. Whether the National Constitution, in defining boundaries between the two, has applied the principle with exact accuracy, is not to be questioned. We are all bound by that defining, without question.

What is now combatted, is the position that secession is *consistent* with the Constitution — is *lawful,* and *peaceful.* It is not contended that there is any express law for it; and nothing should ever be implied as law, which leads to unjust, or absurd consequences. The nation purchased, with money, the countries out of which several of these States were formed. Is it just that they shall go off without leave, and without refunding? The nation paid very large sums, (in the aggregate, I believe, nearly a hundred millions) to relieve Florida of the aboriginal tribes. Is it just that she shall now

be off without consent, or without making any return? The nation is now in debt for money applied to the benefit of these so-called seceding States, in common with the rest. Is it just, either that creditors shall go unpaid, or the remaining States pay the whole? A part of the present national debt was contracted to pay the old debts of Texas. Is it just that she shall leave, and pay no part of this herself?

Again, if one State may secede, so may another; and when all shall have seceded, none is left to pay the debts. Is this quite just to creditors? Did we notify them of this sage view of ours, when we borrowed their money? If we now recognize this doctrine, by allowing the seceders to go in peace, it is difficult to see what we can do, if others choose to go, or to extort terms upon which they will promise to remain.

The seceders insist that our Constitution admits of secession. They have assumed to make a National Constitution of their own, in which, of necessity, they have either *discarded,* or *retained,* the right of secession, as they insist, it exists in ours. If they have discarded it, they thereby admit that, on principle, it ought not to be in ours. If they have retained it, by their own construction of ours they show that to be consistent they must secede from one another, whenever they shall find it the easiest way of settling their debts, or effecting any other selfish, or unjust object. The principle itself is one of disintegration, and upon which no government can possibly endure.

If all the States, save one, should assert the power to *drive* that one out of the Union, it is presumed the whole class of seceder politicians would at once deny the power, and denounce the act as the greatest outrage upon State rights. But suppose that precisely the same act, in stead of being called "driving the one out," should be called "the seceding of the others from that one," it would be exactly what the seceders claim to do; unless, indeed, they make the point, that the one, because it is a minority, may rightfully do, what the others, because they are a majority, may not rightfully do. These politicians are subtle, and profound, on the rights of minorities. They are not partial to that power which made the Constitution, and speaks from the preamble, calling itself "We, the People."

It may well be questioned whether there is, to-day, a majority of the legally qualified voters of any State, except perhaps South Carolina, in favor of disunion. There is much reason to believe that the Union men are the majority in many, if not in every other one, of the so-called seceded States. The contrary has not been demonstrated in any one of them. It is ventured to affirm this, even of Virginia and Tennessee; for the result of an election, held in military camps, where the bayonets are all on one side of the question voted upon, can scarcely be considered as demonstrating popular sentiment. At such an election, all that large class who are, at once, *for* the Union, and *against* coercion, would be coerced to vote against the Union.

It may be affirmed, without extravagance, that the free institutions we enjoy, have developed the powers, and improved the condition, of our whole people, beyond any example in the world. Of this we now have a striking, and an impressive illustration. So large an army as the government has now on foot, was never before known, without a soldier in it, but who had taken his place there, of his own free choice. But more than this: there are many single Regiments whose members, one and other, possess full practical knowledge of all

the arts, sciences, professions, and whatever else, whether useful or elegant, is known in the world; and there is scarcely one, from which there could not be selected, a President, a Cabinet, a Congress, and perhaps a Court, abundantly competent to administer the government itself. Nor do I say this is not true, also, in the army of our late friends, now adversaries, in this contest; but if it is, so much better the reason why the government, which has conferred such benefits on both them and us, should not be broken up. Whoever, in any section, proposes to abandon such a government, would do well to consider, in deference to what principle it is, that he does it — what better he is likely to get in its stead — whether the substitute will give, or be intended to give, so much of good to the people. There are some foreshadowings on this subject. Our adversaries have adopted some Declarations of Independence; in which, unlike the good old one, penned by Jefferson, they omit the words "all men are created equal." Why? They have adopted a temporary national constitution, in the preamble of which, unlike our good old one, signed by Washington, they omit "We, the People," and substitute "We, the deputies of the sovereign and independent States." Why? Why this deliberate pressing out of view, the rights of men, and the authority of the people?

This is essentially a People's contest. On the side of the Union, it is a struggle for maintaining in the world, that form, and substance of government, whose leading object is, to elevate the condition of men — to lift artificial weights from all shoulders — to clear the paths of laudable pursuit for all — to afford all, an unfettered start, and a fair chance, in the race of life. Yielding to partial, and temporary departures, from necessity, this is the leading object of the government for whose existence we contend.

I am most happy to believe that the plain people understand, and appreciate this. It is worthy of note, that while in this, the government's hour of trial, large numbers of those in the Army and Navy, who have been favored with the offices, have resigned, and proved false to the hand which had pampered them, not one common soldier, or common sailor is known to have deserted his flag.

Great honor is due to those officers who remain true, despite the example of their treacherous associates; but the greatest honor, and most important fact of all, is the unanimous firmness of the common soldiers, and common sailors. To the last man, so far as known, they have successfully resisted the traitorous efforts of those, whose commands, but an hour before, they obeyed as absolute law. This is the patriotic instinct of the plain people. They understand, without an argument, that destroying the government, which was made by Washington, means no good to them.

Our popular government has often been called an experiment. Two points in it, our people have already settled — the successful *establishing*, and the successful *administering* of it. One still remains — its successful *maintenance* against a formidable [internal] attempt to overthrow it. It is now for them to demonstrate to the world, that those who can fairly carry an election, can also suppress a rebellion — that ballots are the rightful, and peaceful, successors of bullets; and that when ballots have fairly, and constitutionally, decided, there can be no successful appeal, back to bullets; that there can be no successful appeal, except to ballots themselves, at succeeding elections. Such will be a great lesson of peace; teaching men that what they can-

not take by an election, neither can they take it by a war — teaching all, the folly of being the beginners of a war.

Lest there be some uneasiness in the minds of candid men, as to what is to be the course of the government towards the Southern States, *after* the rebellion shall have been suppressed, the Executive deems it proper to say, it will be his purpose, then, as ever, to be guided by the Constitution, and the laws; and that he probably will have no different understanding of the powers, and duties of the Federal government, relatively to the rights of the States, and the people, under the Constitution, than that expressed in the inaugural address.

He desires to preserve the government, that it may be administered for all, as it was administered by the men who made it. Loyal citizens everywhere, have the right to claim this of their government; and the government has no right to withhold, or neglect it. It is not perceived that, in giving it, there is any coercion, any conquest, or any subjugation, in any just sense of those terms.

The Constitution provides, and all the States have accepted the provision, that "The United States shall guarantee to every State in this Union a republican form of government." But, if a State may lawfully go out of the Union, having done so, it may also discard the republican form of government; so that to prevent its going out, is an indispensable *means*, to the *end*, of maintaining the guaranty mentioned; and when an end is lawful and obligatory, the indispensable means to it, are also lawful, and obligatory.

It was with the deepest regret that the Executive found the duty of employing the war-power, in defence of the government, forced upon him. He could but perform this duty, or surrender the existence of the government. No compromise, by public servants, could, in this case, be a cure; not that compromises are not often proper, but that no popular government can long survive a marked precedent, that those who carry an election, can only save the government from immediate destruction, by giving up the main point, upon which the people gave the election. The people themselves, and not their servants, can safely reverse their own deliberate decisions. As a private citizen, the Executive could not have consented that these institutions shall perish; much less could he, in betrayal of so vast, and so sacred a trust, as these free people had confided to him. He felt that he had no moral right to shrink; nor even to count the chances of his own life, in what might follow. In full view of his great responsibility, he has, so far, done what he has deemed his duty. You will now, according to your own judgment, perform yours. He sincerely hopes that your views, and your action, may so accord with his, as to assure all faithful citizens, who have been disturbed in their rights, of a certain, and speedy restoration of them, under the Constitution, and the laws.

And having thus chosen our course, without guile, and with pure purpose, let us renew our trust in God, and go forward without fear, and with manly hearts.

ABRAHAM LINCOLN

July 4, 1861.

David M. Potter: LINCOLN IN THE SECESSION CRISIS

David M. Potter, Professor of History at Yale University, is one of the leading contemporary students of Lincoln's role in the secession crisis. His study of the political decisions which led to war presents a classic statement of the view that Lincoln bears substantial responsibility for wrecking the efforts to forge a compromise solution to the major issues dividing the North and South. In this selection, Potter examines the possibilities for compromise and presents a critical view of Lincoln's policy.

THREE weeks and two days after the election of Lincoln, every state of the deep South except Louisiana had initiated the process of secession. From the low country of Carolina to the banks of the Mississippi, from the Appalachians to Key West, the states were going methodically about the business of breaking up the Federal Union.

For the Republicans, this marked an hour of decision. The swift-moving developments of the last weeks of 1860 challenged them to recognize at once the proportions of the movement which they confronted, and to determine upon their response to measures of disunion. . . .

Up to the time of Lincoln's election, . . . a faithful Republican could scarcely dally with the idea of compromise without peril to his political soul. The platform said that secession was treason, from which he might infer that compromise was a compact with traitors. Mr. Greeley said that the compromisers were simpletons; Mr. Seward said that they were men of weak virtue or weak nerves;

Mr. Lincoln indicated that they were persons who permitted themselves to be slandered or frightened into desertion of duty. . . . By the year 1860, these attitudes had taken root so firmly as to be virtually a part of the Republican creed. . . .

Despite Republican . . . hostility to the practice of compromise, events were soon to force the question of compromise upon the party. For there existed, outside of party ranks, a tradition of compromise, deep-rooted and powerful. Coeval in origin with the Constitution itself, this policy of compromise had been used to heal every major sectional dispute in the history of the Republic. It reconciled the claims of a slaveholding South and a non-slaveholding North as to the representation of slaves in 1787; it drew the line 36°30′ between these same forces when they contested for control of the Louisiana Territory in 1820; it prevented the collision of Nullification Ordinance and Force Bill in 1833; and it adjusted the conflicting claims which

From David M. Potter, *Lincoln and His Party in the Secession Crisis* (New Haven, Yale University Press, 1942), pp. 46, 49–51, 57–60, 65–66, 68, 112–114, 127, 133, 157–160, 184–186, 188–190, 195, 199–200, 208, 213, 215–218, 375.

racked the country in 1850. For every compromise adopted dozens of others had been proposed, and plans of adjustment sprang up, as if by reflex action, from every violent agitation.

This tradition of compromise was especially powerful in the Border states. There it commanded the primary allegiance of almost all politicians, whatever their party labels might be. The old followers of Henry Clay made conciliation their paramount policy, and it would not be too much to say that they constituted a distinct compromise party. When this party proposed John Bell for the presidency in 1860, with no platform save "the Constitution and the Union," it was with no purpose to shirk the issues of the day, but to stress the complete subordination of these issues to a single-minded policy of saving the Union. Compared with this great objective, all other issues were of negligible importance and would be settled in any way which gave promise of maintaining the Federal relationship.

For the six years prior to Lincoln's election, however, the compromise party had been forced to forego efforts for definitive compromise. The violent antagonism between the sections made legislative agreement virtually impossible. The South brandished the Dred Scott decision and resolved to open all territories to slavery, while Northern majorities supported the Republicans in their policy of complete exclusion. As time passed, the assault on Sumner, Bleeding Kansas, the Lecompton contest, the literary incendiarism of Hinton Helper and Mrs. Stowe, and the raid at Harpers Ferry intensified sectional discord and destroyed every possibility of reconciling divergent sectional policies.

In these circumstances, it was fruitless to propose legislative compromise and none was seriously attempted. But this does not mean that the spirit of compromise had withered under the cross-fire between North and South. It means, rather, that as the conciliators despaired of negotiating an agreement they labored instead to banish the slavery question from Congress, and to elect moderate men to public office. To denationalize the slavery issue, they proposed to leave each territory free to choose for itself, or, as they expressed it, to exercise the right of "popular sovereignty." While thus excluding the slavery issue from the legislative branch of government, they also strove to exclude sectionalism from the executive branch by securing the election to the presidency of men who commanded appreciable support in every part of the country. Thus, many Whigs in 1856 deserted their own candidate, Fillmore, and supported the Democrat, Buchanan, solely for the purpose of defeating Frémont and averting the crisis which his election would have caused. Similarly, the moderates of 1860 gave strenuous support to the campaigns of Bell and Douglas. This *ad hominem* method succeeded, for a time, in forestalling the crisis, and it may well be that the defeat of Frémont had averted a sectional conflict quite as effectively as any of the Clay compromises. But peace maintained on such a basis was little more than an armed truce, for the Union became, in effect, a federalization of two divergent sections under an executive acceptable to both. Should this precarious executive ambidexterity be disturbed, the Union itself would be jeopardized.

The election of Lincoln produced exactly this effect. There were some who hoped to temporize a little longer, reminding the South that she still held a veto in the Senate, and urging that Lincoln be trusted until he should commit an "overt act." But the election itself was overt enough to unloose the fire-eaters, and South Carolina's haste imposed upon the moderates the task of improvising at once a compromise more extensive than any that had been formulated in the previous six decades. Yet hopeless as this seemed, it was made easier, paradoxically, by the same factor which made it necessary — that is, by the very imminence of the crisis. As disunion loomed up, nationalistic pride could be expected to assert itself, and in many cases to override partisan zeal and sectional principles. It was the task of the moderates, therefore, to sponsor measures to evoke the full tide of Union sentiment, while arousing sectional bias as little as possible.

It was their task, more particularly, to win some degree of Republican support. For the Republican party was in every sense at the center of the problem. The crisis was precipitated by Republican victory, and secession resulted from fear of Republican aggressions. Fear thus excited could be allayed, if at all, by none but the Republicans who had aroused it; concessions in the moment of victory could be given by none but the Republicans who had won it; promises of forbearance in the administration could be fulfilled only by the Republicans who would control it; and proposed compromises could be enacted into law or embedded in the Constitution only by legislative majorities which were Republican in the Federal House of Representatives, and in both houses of fourteen of the eighteen free state legislatures. In short, the future lay with the Republicans, and without their active support compromise would be impossible. No proposal of adjustment could have any efficacy except insofar as it secured Republican endorsement. . . .

. . . No conceivable settlement . . . could have conciliated the sections [except one which dealt with] the problem of the status of slavery in the territories. For the whole slavery contest had centered upon the status of the Federal territories. The territorial question had first been raised when a real empire was at stake, and it had continued to dominate political thought even after the issue was limited, in its application, to areas where slavery was already barred by physical environment. But thus reduced to an abstraction, devoid of tangible significance, it retained such emotional potency as a symbol that it remained the point of focus of all the political, economic, and social antagonism of the two sections. The history of the slavery contest was a record of paroxysms arising from territorial rivalry, and of lulls following upon territorial compromise. So invariable was this recurrence that a cycle of slavery agitation had been defined. This cycle always began with the acquisition or opening of new territory. Such an event proved the signal for a conflict between slavery expansionists and exclusionists. As the violence of their contest increased so far as to threaten the security of the country, moderates and Unionists became alarmed and intervened to impose some sort of territorial adjustment, whereupon the excitement diminished and the country lapsed into a period of relative quiet. . . . Inevitably, therefore, in any great national crisis, despairing Unionists would turn once more to the remedy which had, at one time, given peace to the Republic. Further, it was inevitable that the acuteness of the danger would rally many supporters who normally spurned such moderation. Thus the logic of events in 1860 promised that the moderates would once again seek a territorial adjustment. . . .

As late as November, Republican rejection of any territorial compromise seemed perfectly certain. Before the meeting of Congress confusion prevailed, and no strong impulse in favor of concession was evident. . . . But, in the weeks after Congress met, a marked trend toward moderation set in. As the crisis developed, pressure from the conciliatory groups began to grow strong. As the weight of this pressure accumulated, the Republicans found increasing difficulty in holding their ranks firm.

A primary source of weakness in the Republican position, and one which greatly increased the party's vulnerability, was the fact that, although victorious, the Republicans remained a minority group. In all of American history, no President has ever been elected with so small a percentage of the popular vote as Lincoln received in 1860. His vote amounted to 39.9 per cent of the total cast. Thus, his actual strength was not only less than that of any other man who had won the presidency, but it was less than that of most of the major candidates who have failed to win it. When Lincoln ran again, in 1864, McClellan received 44.9 per cent of the vote, and was defeated. And in the campaigns of the ensuing forty years, there was never a time when the defeated candidate could not claim a larger share of public support than Lincoln received in 1860. Not until Parker lost to Roosevelt in 1904, did any major candidate command less strength in losing than Lincoln had commanded in winning.

This minority status inevitably impaired Republican capacity to resist pressure. A clear majority would have armed the party with a "mandate from the people," strengthening their public prestige as well as their moral assurance, and bestowing upon them the ultimate sanction of a democracy. But, lacking this sanction, Lincoln and his party were subjected to an unremitting barrage of demands, especially from Northern Democrats, that they subordinate their minority wishes to the popular desire to conciliate the South. Beginning on November 8, the New York *Herald* took up this cry, and played every variation as the mood suggested. On some days it demanded that Mr. Lincoln release his electors, and relinquish his claim on the presidency; in more reasonable moments, it simply demanded from him a statement with which to reassure the South; again, it demanded conciliatory measures from Seward and the Republicans in Congress, or from the governors of important Northern states. And whether exhorting governors, congressmen, or President-elect, the *Herald* reminded them at regular intervals that they had no majority.

The *Herald,* however, not content merely to emphasize that the 1,865,000 Republican voters were, as a class, in the minority, was also impelled to analyze these voters to show that not all of them were slavery exclusionists. Many had voted as they did to secure a tariff, or to get a homestead, or to rebuke the corruption of the Democratic machine. They had certainly not intended to pursue the anti-slavery cause into the cannon's mouth, and many had never become wholehearted Republicans. According to the *Herald's* plausible estimate, 900,000 of these voters had been conservative Whigs, followers of compromising Henry Clay only a few years before, and another 315,000 were squeamish Democrats who could not stomach the doings of the machine. Half of the Whigs and all of the Democrats, reckoned the *Herald,* were indifferent or hostile to the Chicago Platform. This would leave barely 1,000,000 voters, or less than one-fourth of the electorate, who had voted for the exclusion of slavery, and even these could not be supposed to have any notion of the consequences of their action. Implicitly, the *Herald* posed the question: Was this vote in any sense a mandate to reject compromise and to embark on a program which might result in war? To this query, it responded with a thumping negative.

While the accuracy of the *Herald's* figures may be questioned, the validity of the basic argument is hard to challenge. If the majority against Lincoln was 3 to 2, the majority against the Republican program of slavery exclusion must have been even heavier. Because of this pronounced lack of majority support, the Republicans were at a moral disadvantage in maintaining their program, and they were perhaps more susceptible than they would admit to demands that they abandon their partisan platform. . . .

With all this storm of pressure which beat upon the Republican party, it is natural that lines began to waver. For a minority party which knew itself to be a minority party, the force of demands from the divided majority in opposition, from the pitifully sincere Border Unionists, and from the importunate financiers, must have seemed almost irresistible. Perhaps the remarkable thing is that the Republican lines did not buckle completely. . . .

The individual congressman was ill fortified to resist all the pressure upon him, and he was especially ill prepared to resist it alone. The Chicago Platform was not without value in his eyes, but it

was, after all, only a campaign document, and the campaign was over. In the absence of a re-statement of policy, or an assumption of responsibility by a leader, he would hesitate to assume the responsibility of defeating compromise. He had waited five weeks for such leadership, and it had not been forthcoming. As time passed, he found his constituents more clamorous for compromise, and his colleagues more receptive to it. In these premises, he must inevitably view it with increasing complaisance.

But whether most Republican congressmen would soon have accepted compromise must remain in the realm of speculation. For the growing tendency was not permitted to continue uninterrupted. From the first . . . the President-elect had followed . . . proceedings apprehensively. It is evident that his apprehension increased with the unfolding of events. In consequence he abandoned his policy of remaining inactive until his inauguration, and quietly but effectively he brought the vast weight of his influence to bear. Assuming a momentous responsibility, he intervened to arrest the growing sentiment for compromise among the Republicans in Congress. . . .

Probably the first overt manifestation of Lincoln's new policy is to be found in a letter of *December 10,* to his close friend *Lyman Trumbull.* It is not certain whether Trumbull applied for advice, or whether Lincoln offered it on his own initiative, but even if it were true that his advice had been solicited, the tone of Lincoln's letter shows that he was not hesitant in assuming leadership. He began this letter abruptly: "Let there be no compromise on the question of extending slavery. If there be, all our labor is lost, and, ere long, must be done again. The dangerous ground — that into which some of our friends have a hankering to run — is Pop[ular] Sov[ereignty]. Have none of it. Stand firm. The tug has to come, and better now than at any time hereafter."

Having once taken the step of intervention in this congressional matter, Lincoln followed up his first note by striking two more blows against compromise in the House of Representatives. William Kellogg and Elihu B. Washburne, who were members of the Illinois delegation in the House, both wrote to Lincoln, evidently requesting his counsel, and thus enabling him to advise them without seeming officious. He replied to Kellogg on the day after his note to Trumbull, and the language of this second note closely paralleled that of the first. Beginning, "Entertain no proposition for a compromise in regard to the extension of slavery," he reiterated his conviction that a compromise would leave all the labor of the Republicans to be done over again, his fear that the doctrine of popular sovereignty might mislead some of his party, and his readiness to face "the tug" at once, rather than later. After a lapse of two more days, a letter from Washburne gave him occasion to repeat essentially the same precepts and the same warnings. This time, he cautioned against the Missouri line, as well as the popular sovereignty formula; once more, he asserted that a territorial compromise would leave the whole contest to be waged over again; and he closed by exhorting Washburne to "hold firm, as with a chain of steel." Thus, for a third time in four days, the President-elect wrote to congressmen of his party, urging them to resist all compromise on the territorial question.

For a time, Lincoln expressed his emphatic views only in private communications to personal friends. But, as time passed, he became less reticent and re-sorted increasingly to more public expressions. This tendency became evident when, on December 17, he sent a message to Thurlow Weed to be transmitted to a conference of Republican governors who were planning to meet in New York. "Should the . . . Governors . . . seem desirous to know my views . . . ," wrote Lincoln, "tell them you judge from my speeches that I will be inflexible on the territorial question; that I probably think either the Missouri line extended, or Douglas's and Eli Thayer's popular sovereignty, would lose us everything we gain by the election; that filibustering for all South of us and making slave States of it would follow, in spite of us, in either case; also that I probably think all opposition, real and apparent, to the fugitive-slave clause of the Constitution ought to be withdrawn."

In this statement, Lincoln still showed a notable degree of reticence in expressing his views. He still stated his opinion only to a semi-private group, and he placed his words in the mouth of a spokesman. But, within a few days more, he completed the transition, and permitted the issuance of a public statement which was clearly authorized. This pronouncement appeared in the New York *Tribune* of December 22: "We are enabled to state in the most positive terms," it said, "that Mr. Lincoln is utterly opposed to any concession or compromise that shall yield one iota of the position occupied by the Republican Party on the subject of slavery in the territories, and that he stands now, as he stood on May last, when he accepted the nomination for the Presidency, square upon the Chicago platform."

After this announcement in the *Tribune,* no one could fail to understand that Lincoln was unalterably opposed to territorial compromise. The firmness of his personal conviction emerged as distinctly as words could state it. . . .

. . . Lincoln's intervention was a vital one. . . . Republican solidarity in rejecting compromise in mid-January marked a complete reversal of the tendency of mid-December, when conciliatory measures seemed to be steadily gaining Republican adherents. . . . Yet the crisis was no less ominous, and the pressure from conciliationist groups had not abated. The change in temper, therefore, resulted from no amelioration in crisis conditions, but from new forces at work within the party. These forces may have been multiple, but certainly none was more potent than the intervention of Lincoln. Almost unobserved, except in the most limited circles, the President-elect had held the ranks of his party solid. . . .

In the problem of the secession crisis, all disputed questions of personal or sectional justification signify far less than the basic, undisputed fact that the public men of 1861 failed to effect the voluntary perpetuation of the Union. In a larger sense, this breakdown of peace began with the sectional antagonism of the preceding decades. In a more immediate sense, it ensued from the condition that no compromise — and, explicitly, no territorial compromise — was either offered by one section or requested by the other.

In the analysis of this failure, attention naturally focuses upon the manner in which Lincoln and his party resisted territorial adjustment. . . . A major question remains as to whether the Republicans defeated a . . . publicly approved device for the maintenance of the Union. . . . If it be true, or if the data indicate, that the compromise proposals were desired by the Unionist states, . . . then the accountability of the Republicans must be regarded as very grave. If, on the other hand, the Crittenden proposals and others like them faced insuperable obstacles from the beginning, in the form of public disapproval . . . then the policy of the Republicans cannot be regarded as being, in any sense, decisive. . . .

Neither polls nor straw votes existed to record the shifting currents of public opinion in the sixties. Nevertheless, it is necessary to read such gauges as were available to determine whether or not that opinion predominantly favored a territorial compromise. Among the evidence which bears on this question, none is more complete and more revealing than the popular vote in the election of 1860. For this vote shows plainly that a majority, not only of the voters as a whole, but even of the voters in states which remained loyal to the Union, regarded the exclusion of slavery from the territories as non-essential or even undesirable, and voted against the candidate who represented this policy. When Lincoln was inaugurated, the states which accepted him as President were states which had cast a majority of more than half a million votes against him, and even when the outbreak of war caused four more states to join the Confederacy, the remaining Union still contained a population in which the majority of the electorate had opposed the Republican ticket. Inasmuch as this majority was divided between Breckinridge, who denied the right of congressional intervention in the territories, Douglas, who offered popular sovereignty as a solution, and Bell, who favored anything that would insure harmony, it appears that the proponents of slavery exclusion lacked a majority, even before the secession crisis.

How far they fell short of attaining a majority is uncertain, but clearly their numerical strength was appreciably less than that of the Republican party as a whole. For many of the citizens who cast their ballots for Lincoln, did so in spite of, rather than because of, his advocacy of slavery exclusion. It is a well known fact that the platform of 1860 made a clever and successful bid for the support of protectionists, advocates of free homesteads, and promoters of a transcontinental railway. Add to this the strength which the Democratic party forfeited through its corruption and that which Lincoln gained simply as a man of the people, and the intrinsic strength of the slavery exclusion program seems very indeterminate, indeed. Honest Abe, the rail-splitter, probably ran fully as strong at the polls as Abraham Lincoln, the friend of the enslaved.

If the advocates of slavery exclusion did not command a majority at the outset of the crisis, they certainly never possessed one thereafter, for it is an incontestable fact that many Republicans who had endorsed the entire Chicago Platform during the campaign, hastily modified their position as the secession crisis developed. Copious evidence proves that defections occurred on a large scale. In Massachusetts, for instance, a number of local elections took place in early December, and in these contests the heavy Republican majorities of the preceding month were heavily reversed in such important towns as Worcester and Newburyport. Where no actual reversal took place, the proportion of Republican strength was reduced, as in Boston, Charlestown, and Lowell. . . .

When the faction of Republican moderates is added to that of Breckinridge Democrats, Douglas Democrats, and Constitutional Unionists, assurance seems doubly certain that the majority opinion of the Unionist states would readily have offered concessions in the territories if thereby they could have secured the perpetuation of the Union. Testimony as to the desire of the majority for compromise is voluminous. . .

. . . but, perhaps, two . . . general observations will suffice. One comes from the pen of that zealous Republican and slavery exclusionist, Horace Greeley, who, some years after the crisis, expressed his belief that the advocates of the Crittenden Compromise had, "with good reason, claimed a large majority of the people in its favor," and that, if it had been submitted to a popular vote, many Republicans "would have refrained from voting at all, while their adversaries would have brought every man to the polls in its support, and carried it by hundreds of thousands." The other comment is that of James Ford Rhodes, who had no disposition to underestimate Republican strength, but who nevertheless concluded that "no doubt can now exist, and but little could have existed in January 1861, that if it [the Crittenden plan] had been submitted to the people, it would have carried the Northern States by a great majority [and] . . . that it would have obtained the vote of almost every man in the border States." If these conclusions are valid, as the preponderance of evidence indicates, it means that when Lincoln moved to defeat compromise, he did not move as the champion of democracy, but as a partisan leader.

In order to achieve any compromise, two conditions are essential: one party must agree to offer concessions, and the other must agree to accept them. Therefore, unless the South wanted compromise and would have accepted it, it would be fallacious to regard Republican refusal to offer terms as equivalent to Republican defeat of compromise proposals. If the secessionists *per se*, with their hatred of the Union, and the Southern nationalists, with their dream of a separate Southern destiny, represented

Southern sentiment, then compromise aspirations were at all times illusory. Thus, a final evaluation of the merit of Republican policy must rest upon a consideration of the temper of the Southern groups with whom the Republicans had to deal. . . .

At no time during the winter of 1860–1861 was secession desired by a majority of the people of the slave states. In proof of this, it is only necessary to cite the miserable failure, until after the war began, of the secession program in Arkansas, Missouri, Kentucky, Tennessee, Maryland, Delaware, Virginia, and North Carolina. Furthermore, secession was not basically desired even by a majority in the lower South, and the secessionists succeeded less because of the intrinsic popularity of their program than because of the extreme skill with which they utilized an emergency psychology, the promptness with which they invoked unilateral action by individual states, and the firmness with which they refused to submit the question of secession to popular referenda. . . .

. . . Even in these circumstances, however, the opposition which they encountered was stubborn and the margin of their success was far more narrow than the later solidarity of the Confederacy indicated. In every one of the Gulf states, except South Carolina, secession was accomplished only after a sharp contest, and even in the Palmetto State, Unionist elements were far stronger than they appeared to be. Without examining these state contests in detail, it will suffice to note certain basic facts. First, in the election of delegates to the conventions, the moderates fought hard against immediate secessionists. For the most part, the election returns for these contests are not available, or do not lend themselves to exact interpretation. But in cases where

tentative analyses are possible, the opposition to immediate secession consistently appears substantial. After the elections in South Carolina and Florida, Mississippi elected her secession convention on December 20. In a total of 41,000 votes cast, nearly 12,000 are not subject to analysis. Of the remainder, 16,874 were cast in favor of immediate secessionists and 12,218 against them. Four days later, in the Alabama election, the opponents of immediate secession cast a vote estimated at 28,181, but 35,693 ballots were against them. Georgia went to the polls on January 2, and registered a decision in favor of immediate secession by a vote of 50,243 to 37,123. Five days in the wake of Georgia, Louisiana indicated a similar preference, on the same question, by a vote of 20,448 to 17,296. If these figures err seriously, it is apparently on the side of the separationists. But, even accepting them at face value, they show the strength of the moderates and the weakness of the secessionists in two striking aspects: first, in each one of the states in question, the foes of immediate secession are credited with at least 42 per cent of the determinable vote; second, in not one case did the precipitationists secure a vote large enough to have constituted a majority of the vote cast by the state in the presidential election of a few weeks earlier.

Apart from the popular election of the conventions, the strength of the moderates was again manifested within the conventions themselves. . . . The secessionists were in the ascendancy by a margin of only 9 delegates out of 69 in Florida, of only 9 out of 99 in Alabama, and of only 36 out of 296 in Georgia. A reversal of 5 votes in Florida, 5 in Alabama, and 19 in Georgia would have gone far to arrest the whole secession movement.

In each of these sharp contests, the secessionists had one great advantage: they could assert, without contradiction, that there remained no hope of receiving guarantees from the Republicans. . . .

In a period of nine days between January 9 and 18, the four states of Mississippi, Florida, Alabama, and Georgia adopted ordinances of secession. In each of these states, a group of conservatives fought against disunion vigorously, and, in three states, almost successfully. They waged these contests under a fatal handicap: they could show no offer of compromise, nor even a gesture of good will from the party which was about to take control of the Federal government. When the secessionists said "The argument is exhausted. All hope of relief in the Union . . . is extinguished," or "All further looking to the North for security for your Constitutional rights in the Union ought to be instantly abandoned," the conservatives had no effective reply, and without it, pleaded the cause of Union in vain. Had they been armed with a reply, they could scarcely have failed to gain the narrow margin of strength which would have enabled them to uphold the Union.

It was the tragedy of the Southern state-rights Unionists — perhaps the basic tragedy of the war — that they were not supported by adequate assurances of the good will and the equitable purpose of the national Unionists of the North. Intrinsically valueless as territorial concession would have been, it would have served as a symbol of Northern recognition of Southern parity in the Union and would have strengthened Southern Unionists immeasurably. Preponderantly, citizens of the North were willing to make such a concession for such a purpose, but Republican partisan leadership prevented this gesture. . . .

In the months that followed [the outbreak of war], Lincoln exhibited great forbearance and charity toward the South. That he did so may not be entirely a consequence of his personal magnanimity. It may also have derived from a conviction that, if the matter had been handled differently — if, indeed, he had handled the matter differently — the conflict might have been averted.

Kenneth M. Stampp: THE REPUBLICAN PARTY IN THE SECESSION CRISIS

Kenneth Stampp's interest in the Civil War crisis is primarily that of an analyst of human behavior. For two decades, Stampp has been teaching and writing about Civil War history. He is one of the nation's outstanding Civil War historians. In this selection, Stampp describes the pressures which beat upon Republican leaders during the secession crisis and sketches the pattern of beliefs which influenced them to choose a policy "which led to war."

AFTER the election of 1860, Republican leaders had an experience that was almost unique in the annals of American politics. Ordinarily, victorious parties have been taunted by their rivals for their subsequent betrayal of promises made in platforms and campaign oratory. During the secession winter, however, Republican politicians chose to stand by the commitments they had made at the Chicago convention: to check the further spread of slavery, to admit Kansas as a free state, to increase the tariff, to pass a homestead act, and to subsidize internal improvements. And their reward was an equal measure of abuse from contemporary opponents and more recent critics for their "obstinate adherence to a mere party platform," their refusal "to sink the partisan into the patriot." But if they had pursued another course and repudiated their previous pledges, presumably they would have been accused of the insincerity and opportunism of time-serving politicians. History had entrapped the Republicans in a moral dilemma!

Why were the adherents of Lincoln so fastidious at this particular time about their political integrity? That is a question which permits no simple explanation. Perhaps a few of the Republicans actually made opposition to compromise a matter of high principle, sincerely believed in the essential wisdom and justice of their party's program, and had no feelings of guilt or responsibility for the secession crisis. The mental rigidity of these "doctrinaires" may have been incomprehensible or offensive to practical politicians whose minds were more flexible, but the "doctrinaires" were nevertheless a group to be reckoned with among the Republicans of 1860.

In those early years the Republican party was not yet completely fettered by machines whose only rule was expediency. Originally it had absorbed in its complex body much of the political wing of a great crusade, namely, the antislavery radicals who had fused the remnants of the Liberty and Free-Soil parties with the new organization. Their hostility to slavery and the southern way of life was a partial expression of the broader nineteenth-century middle-class liberalism

Reprinted from *And the War Came*, by Kenneth M. Stampp, pp. 147–158, by permission of the Louisiana State University Press. Copyright 1950 by the Louisiana State University Press.

which they espoused. They put their faith in individual freedom, in the right of each man to the fruits of his enterprise. They placed their hope in the "music of the loom," in the material progress and abundance they foresaw in a nation of shopkeepers, mechanics, and free farmers. Actually they had simply adapted to the realities of the northern milieu the economic creed of Adam Smith and the English Manchester School. To its propagation they brought an intense degree of moral fervor. In a very real sense it was this group which gave the Republicans their *raison d'être*, their driving force, and their only common principle, namely, opposition to slavery expansion. Without these men it is doubtful that the party could have survived.

The radicals had endured too much, bolted the major parties and supported forlorn hopes too often, stood outside the gates of power too long, to permit any doubt of their devotion to principle. For such representatives of the antislavery crusade as Charles Sumner, Joshua R. Giddings, Owen Lovejoy, and George W. Julian to have yielded anything to the Slave Power after the victory had finally been won was unthinkable. They *believed* in the doctrine of the "irrepressible conflict" and denied that it could be removed by any feasible compromise; they insisted that their platform, so far from being sectional, actually contained the only true formula for national well-being. Republicans stood by their principles, explained one, simply "because *they know their principles to be essential to the welfare and even to the very existence of the Union.*" James Russell Lowell encompassed the thoughts of this group precisely:

. . . It is quite time that it should be understood that freedom is also an institution deserving some attention in a Model Republic, that a decline in stocks is more tolerable and more transient than one in public spirit, and that material prosperity was never known to abide long in a country that had lost its political morality. The fault of the Free States in the eyes of the South is not one that can be atoned for by any yielding of special points here and there. Their offence is that they are free, and that their habits and prepossessions are those of Freedom. Their crime is the census of 1860. Their increase in numbers, wealth, and power is a standing aggression. It would not be enough to please the Southern States that we should stop asking them to abolish slavery, — what they demand of us is nothing less than that we should abolish the spirit of the age. . . . It is time that the South should learn . . . that the difficulty of the Slavery question is slavery itself, — nothing more, nothing less. It is time that the North should learn that it has nothing left to compromise but the rest of its self-respect.

Still, granting the depth and sincerity of their convictions, was it not possible that these "doctrinaires" in refusing to yield on the issue of slavery expansion were contending for a mere abstraction? Certainly a plausible case could be made to show that none of the existing territories was suitable to slavery and the plantation system, that the radicals therefore were endangering the Union over a meaningless point of honor. Representative Daniel E. Somes of Maine, while hardly answering the question, made the most obvious reply by turning the point against the South: "You say it is a mere abstraction for which we are contending, because slavery cannot possibly go there. And yet you regard this abstraction of so much importance to you that you say you are willing to dissolve the Union . . . to secure it. If it is an abstraction with us, of course it must be an abstraction with you." But the fact of the matter was that, rightly or wrongly, many in both sections believed that the issue had substance to it. There was still the vivid memory of the recent struggle in Kansas, the reality of a comprehensive slave code in the Territory of New Mexico; and there was the very live problem of whether slavery was to enter the future territories that Manifest Destiny seemed to promise to the expanding Americans. Finally, in a broader sense this "point of honor," this "abstraction," was but a symbol of the many basic issues which divided the sections; for slavery expansion, after all, was only one facet of the "irrepressible conflict." And symbols are exceedingly important in a struggle between rival ideologies and rival social patterns.

In addition to the radical moralizing on the penalties of deserting eternal principles, Republicans offered a more specific rationale for their refusal to back down. They asserted, for example, that their opponents did not ask for a compromise (which involves a mutual give-and-take) but only for a one-sided yielding on the part of the North. Yet the North also had grievances to be considered if there were to be a general adjustment of sectional relationships. For one thing, Northerners demanded protection from proslavery mobs when traveling in the South and the repeal of state laws which imprisoned Negro seamen when their ships stopped at southern ports. In addition they insisted that revisions would have to be made in the fugitive-slave law before northern personal-liberty laws were repealed: jury trials and other safeguards would have to be provided to prevent the return of free Negroes. Above all, a *sine qua non* of any settlement must be southern recognition of the perpetuity of the Union, a dis-

avowal of the right of secession. As one Republican phrased it: "Let us hereafter know beyond a doubt that we have a government. What will compromise amount to if a state can secede at will[?]"

But Southerners showed no desire to grant any of these; not even the politicians of the upper South would deny the legality of secession. What was required of the North, in fact, was not a compromise but a complete surrender. "Allow the South to govern this country, and you would reach the real difficulty," protested an indignant Yankee; no other terms would satisfy her. Secessionists, opined a correspondent of Trumbull, ". . . will be satisfied with nothing less than the repeal of our Revenue Laws, of our Navigation Laws, of our Fishing Bounties, — in fact of all legislation that is not demanded by the wants of the peculiar interests of the South. They complain of the political and commercial supremacy of the North, and will be content with nothing less than a reduction of their more prosperous neighbor to their own level." The end result of further concessions must be the utter humiliation and subordination of every northern interest. If the North temporized, explained Wade, Southerners would "consider it a victory and become ten times more insolent than ever." In the opinion of another Republican, any yielding would virtually assure the South that "Whenever you are beaten at the ballot-box you have only to steal the public property and declare war against the Government, and we will make concessions. . . ." Representative Orris S. Ferry of Connecticut drew a startling picture of the future:

. . . Suppose we yield; sacrifice the moral convictions of the North, and the revolted

States return to their allegiance: the tariff bill . . . is taken from the table of the Senate and passed; forthwith the hosts of sedition are rallied, secession again raises its hideous front, and amid the clangor of arms sounding from the Gulf, the industrial interests of the nation are immolated upon the altars of treason. . . . After peace has been restored by the new surrender, the homestead bill is reached upon the Calendar of the Senate, guns roar from Fort Moultrie, bayonets bristle at Pensacola, batteries are planted on the banks of the Mississippi, and amid shouts of "compromise" the Government yields once more, and the free emigrant of every section is sacrificed to the plantation.

Equally frightening to the nationalists was the dangerous example of surrendering to rebels in arms, of placing a premium upon rebellion which could easily lead to national suicide. With this as a precedent a pattern might be established which would be followed thereafter by the defeated party in every national election. Any bargaining with Southerners would be a practical recognition of the right of secession, and that would make a mockery of the authority of the Federal government. In essence the Union would be lost as surely as if the independence of the South were conceded at once. "I am afraid to compromise," confessed a Republican, "for fear of demoralizing the government." In short, compromise, so far from being a remedy for disunion, would only aggravate the evil. "Instead of healing the disease, concession will make that disease constitutional, chronic, and fatal." A "patching up" would only "postpone the evil day"; it would bequeath to the future an issue that would still one day have to be faced.

Republicans also bolstered their case by citing the past conduct and present attitude of the South. In the past the Southerners had allegedly violated every

compromise that had been made. "We can make no compromise that will be more binding or conclusive than that which secured the admission of Missouri," asserted the New York *Tribune*, "yet that Compromise, which was effected by an almost unanimous vote of the South, was repudiated by a like vote within the next quarter of a century." "No more compromises with the covenant-breakers!" insisted another. "Not another concession from freedom to the treacherous south." Sumner argued bitterly, *"They are all essentially false, with treason in their hearts, if not on their tongues."*

Finally, it was easiest of all to present the evidence that secessionists had no desire to receive concessions from the North. This was a constantly recurring theme in Republican speeches and newspapers; it seemed convincing because of such incidents as the manifesto of the thirty southern congressmen to their constituents and such statements as those of fire-eaters like Wigfall. After the Deep South had refused to attend the Peace Conference, Thad Stevens could declaim with an air of finality: "Thus ends negotiation; thus ends concession; thus ends compromise, by the solemn declaration of the seceding party that they will not listen to concession or compromise." Ironically but inevitably, the refusal of one side to entertain an adjustment, and of the other to offer it, provided reciprocal advantages for the policy of the dominant political group in each section.

One other factor helped to shape the course of the compromise battle: party politics. In the last analysis the issue was settled in Congress by a group of professional politicians who, according to the normal standards of their trade, attached much significance to considerations of personal and party gain. To deny that many northern congressmen adjusted their views about conciliation to the requirements of political expediency would be to overlook one of the functional concepts of the American party system. Through the minds of these politicians, believed the New York *World*, always ran the question, "How shall the republican party be annihilated, or preserved [?] . . . On all sides there seems to exist this selfishness of party. . . ."

Indeed this opportunism was not the responsibility of any one faction, for the Democrats were just as solicitous of party interests as were the Republicans. Unquestionably the Democrats felt most keenly the political consequences of compromise failure and secession, for with the South out of the Union their power was substantially weakened. Moreover, in a narrower sense, the Democrats strove for the advantage of portraying themselves as the would-be saviors of the Union and their opponents as a standing menace to its survival. In effect they invited the Republican party to abandon its platform, "repent of its iniquities, reform its policy," and confess that it had "thus far proceeded upon false pretenses of morality and philanthropy. . . ." More precisely, Republicans were urged to disband. What Douglas men really hoped for, complained a Lincoln paper, was that the Republican party would "destroy itself" so that the Democratic party might be "reconstructed on its ruins."

During the secession crisis, Democrats lost no opportunity to foster disunity in the ranks of their rivals or to mock them when they showed any signs of weakening. Thus Douglas chided the Republicans in Congress for allegedly adopting his platform when they voted to organize the territories of Colorado, Nevada, and Dakota without forcing a restriction upon slavery. To Senator Henry Wilson this furnished proof of the hypocrisy of Douglas' professed nonpartisanship and evidence that his primary aim was to rebuild "the broken ranks of the Democracy." The New York *Times* when it opposed the immediate passage of the Wilmot Proviso was rewarded with tart sarcasm from the Democratic Boston *Post:* "Verily the work goes bravely on! . . . Mischief has done its work! The storm is raised! Still here is more backing down. It is good to see repentance." As a result the *Times* complained bitterly that conciliatory Republicans were "taunted with tardy cowardice and with a disposition to abandon their party. . . . The hypocritical insincerity of these [Democratic] appeals for compromise . . . is becoming too glaring to deceive any portion of the community much longer."

But while Democrats coveted the political profit from splitting their opponents and promoting appeasement, Republicans looked upon compromise as the shortest route to political suicide. It would necessarily have required a repudiation of their platform, especially their one common principle of opposition to slavery expansion; it would have been a virtual admission that southern complaints were valid, that the Republican victory at the polls justified southern secession; and it would have involved a disastrous public humiliation. A terrible fear of these consequences ran through the speeches and writings of numerous Republican leaders. Over and over they droned that a Republican who favored compromise would simply furnish "proof that he is *scared,*" that he would achieve "the annihilation of the party," that he would promote "the re-establishment in power of the Democratic party," or that he virtually confessed that "Republican-ism is a 'dead dog.'" Representative Cadwalladar C. Washburn of Wisconsin was even convinced that the bill to admit New Mexico was a conspiracy to weaken the Republicans by adding two more proslavery senators to the upper cham-ber. To another Republican the whole compromise movement was simply a "plott [*sic*] by the slave holders and democrats to regain control of the Federal Government." Weed, during his visit to Washington in January, found his party friends obsessed with this dread.

Panicky Republicans had before them a lesson from the Whigs, who, many be-lieved, had been wrecked by compromise a decade before. "Beware of Compro-mise," ran a typical admonishment. "It killed Clay and Webster. It killed the old Whig party, and if you are not care-ful it will slaughter the present genera-tion of politicians." The inevitable result would have been fragmentation because antislavery Republicans would not toler-ate concessions; they would have quit the organization first. Radicals warned that those who had been "educated by the Kansas tyrannies" meant "to stand firmly by this [antislavery] principle, cutting loose from any party that deserts it." Giddings' newspaper promised that if the Republican party yielded, "we will repudiate it with a full heart, and counsel all our friends to do the same. We have degraded ourselves enough." Thus it was all too evident that reunion through com-promise was impossible without the death of the Republican party, and there were few of its members who chose to make that sacrifice.

Yet it would be wrong to assume that most Republicans *consciously* placed party considerations above peaceful re-union. Even those not properly classified among the "doctrinaires" generally would

have denied that their chief concern was the salvation of their party and would have insisted that their solicitude was for the well-being of the whole nation. Representative Somes of Maine gave an exceptionally clear illustration of the way concepts of party advantage and public weal were often fused in the politician's mind. "In a new country like ours," he told his colleagues, "where everything is yet undeveloped, . . . the bold and coura-geous are bound to succeed, while the timid will complainingly follow after them." Hence he commended to Repub-licans a course of boldness and rectitude, for "I would save this young champion of freedom and true democracy — the Republican party — from internal dissen-sion and dissolution."

There was still another factor which mitigated the seeming crassness of Re-publicans weighing the effects of com-promise on the scale of party gain. Their attitude posed the general problem of political responsibility. Whatever others may have desired, Republican voters overwhelmingly opposed concessions. Consequently, to say that compromise would have destroyed the Republican party is simply to say that the congress-men who supported it would have been repudiated by the party rank and file.

More than that, it was quite evident that the dissolution of the Republican organization would merely have paved the way for the formation of a new north-ern antislavery party which would have resumed the fight against the Slave Power. The elimination of the Republi-can party would neither have produced political harmony nor have removed the fundamental causes of sectional conflict. The radical Free-Soil Republicans made it incontrovertibly clear that they would build another party before yielding any of their principles. Many of Sumner's friends hinted that it might be necessary "to fight the battle all over again," or that "by a new 'bolt' . . . the fight with the Slave Power must be begun anew." "I helped to make the Republican party," vowed William H. Herndon, Lincoln's abolitionist law partner, "and if it forsakes its distinctive ideas, I can help to tear it down, and help to erect a new party that shall never cower to any slave driver." Representative John F. Potter of Wisconsin believed that there were enough of the faithful left "to form a nucleus for a genuine republican party, should the conservative influence in the present one destroy or demoralize us." And Owen Lovejoy laughed at the talk of reorganizing the Republican party with the radicals excluded: "I wish you a merry time of it my masters. A very interesting play, Hamlet with Hamlet left out!"

And this tentative discussion of a new sectional party only provided further proof that there were certain basic sectional issues which could not be compromised away. The champions of appeasement were always breaking their lances on the tough realities of the "irrepressible conflict." They could neither silence the northern antislavery radicals nor prevent them from prosecuting their fight through political action. Much less could they devise constitutional amendments which would obliterate the chronic antagonisms between agrarian and industrial economies. At best the work of the northern compromisers was superficial; at worst it was fraudulent.

Avery Craven: LINCOLN AND THE ROAD TO WAR

Avery Craven is one of the foremost historians of the Civil War period. This brief excerpt from his study of The Coming of the Civil War *deals with Lincoln's decision to send provisions to reinforce Fort Sumter. It presents a critical analysis of this decision in the light of alternatives available to Lincoln.*

WHEN Lincoln left Springfield to take over the presidency of a crumbling republic, three courses of action were open to him. He might continue the watchful-waiting policy of his predecessor, hold the Border States, and hope for a reaction which would bring the "erring sisters" back to the Union and the nation to peace. It would not be a popular or a promising way. It would require withdrawal from the forts in Confederate territory and a gradual, if not admitted, yielding of Republican principles. It might end only in the permanent establishment of the new Confederate government. It had already ruined James Buchanan. It might destroy Lincoln and his party. Yet, if the nation were saved and a civil war averted, it might be worth the trial and the cost.

A second course was that of complete surrender by compromises sweeping enough to satisfy the now aggressive South. That would immediately wreck the Republican Party and sacrifice all that the campaign and the years behind it meant. Even if the South accepted, all the problems and sentiments which had produced this crisis would remain. Yet who could say that these problems were not gradually solving themselves? The territorial conflict was certainly over; even slavery might, from natural causes, be on its way out. Who was wise enough to forecast the future?

The third course was that of action. Lincoln could refuse to accept the fact of secession, hold the forts, collect the revenues, and enforce the law. Andrew Jackson had succeeded with such a policy. The strong conservative element in the Lower South would assent; the Border States would approve. The only difficulty was one of managing public opinion so as to keep it on the government's side. An appeal to Union sentiments, to the old national traditions, would prepare the way. The rash actions of the hotheads in the seceded states would furnish the excuse for action. The same vague talk which permitted listeners to understand what it suited them to understand would accomplish the rest. Party and nation — now one in values — might be saved at a minimum cost of force.

Whether Lincoln thought all this out or not we do not know. Some things indicate that he did. Yet his talk and his actions were not always concise and

Reprinted from Avery Craven, *The Coming of the Civil War* (Chicago: University of Chicago Press, 1957), pp. 435–439. Reprinted by permission of the author.

direct. He hesitated and fumbled to a degree, but he did act, and action quickly set him along the third course. As he turned eastward, he stated a program, in questions at Indianapolis, which seemed harmless to the North, but which instantly alarmed the South. ". . . Whatever may have been the motive which suggested the Indianapolis harangues," said the Nashville *Patriot*, "there can be no mistake as to one thing, and that is they prove him to be a narrow-minded Republican partisan incapable apparently of rising to the attitude of statesmanship necessary to a thorough comprehension of the national crisis, and the remedies demanded by patriotism to preserve the government he has been selected to administer. . . ." ". . . It is a war proposition couched in language intended to conceal the enormity of the crime beneath pretexts too absurd to require exposure and fallacies too flimsy to deceive the most stupid," commented the Louisville *Daily Courier*. In Washington, he launched a series of secret intrigues for the holding of the Southern forts which staggered the staid and careful navy and military men who had been in charge. Agreements between local officials and garrisons were ignored. Ships, disguised and sometimes flying the British flag, were dispatched on secret missions with men and supplies. The unofficial assurances given to Southern agents by Seward were repudiated and a set of conditions created which made the actual firing on Fort Sumter by alarmed and enraged Southerners almost a foregone conclusion.

Whether these acts were part of a well-worked-out policy of accepting what seemed to be an irrepressible conflict, and cleverly throwing the responsibility for beginning the war onto the South for the psychological advantage, or whether they were the result of blundering along with the sweep of events, we cannot say with complete assurance. We do know that, with Lincoln's assumption of control, a firmer, uncompromising temper marked the policy of the Federal government. There was constant talk of yielding after a respectable show of force, but no definite assurance of action. Fort Sumter, in the harbor of Charleston, South Carolina, the most dangerous spot in all the troubled nation, was made the point of decision. Acting under orders directly from the President, in the face of sound warnings that such a move meant war, Captain Fox, one April day, set out from New York harbor with ships and provisions for the relief of the Federal troops still holding that fort. On April 12, the Confederate troops stationed about the harbor opened fire, thereby "forcing" Lincoln to call for troops for the suppression of rebellion.

A few days later, Lincoln consoled Captain Fox for his failure to reach and relieve the fort, by writing: "You and I both anticipated that the course of the country would be advanced by making the attempt to provision Fort Sumter, even if it should fail; and it is no small consolation now to feel that our anticipation is justified by the result." Not long after this letter was written, he boasted to his friend Orville H. Browning that: ". . . He himself conceived the idea, and proposed sending supplies, without an attempt to reinforce giving notice to Gov. Pickens of S. C. The plan succeeded. They attacked Sumter — it fell, and thus, did more service than it otherwise could."

With the call for troops to subdue their fellow Southerners, the conservative element in the Border States lost their hold. Two days later, Virginia went out, then North Carolina, Arkansas, and Tennessee, leaving Maryland, Kentucky, and Missouri divided into local warring factions. As those who had refused to allow emotions to overrule their minds gave way, one of them spoke for the sanity of his age and of all time: "I am impotent to do anything which my judgment and conscience approve. I cannot avert the war, consistent with the re-establishment of a government so good as that we pull down. Whilst I cannot hesitate where no choice is left, only to fight for the South and home, or for the North, if I should fall in such a contest, I would find in a dying hour no comfort in the conviction that I had sacrificed my life in a *just* cause. It is true that I believe that Lincoln had no right to call out the militia, make War and blockade the ports. . . . If the restoration of the Union was his object, which I believe was his object, then he is a fool. If his purpose was to drive off all the Slave states, in order to make war on them and annihilate Slavery, then he is a Devil and in the latter supposition I could fight with a hearty good will. . . . My maxim has always been to choose among the evils around me and do the best I can. I think the annals of the world furnish no instance of so groundless a war — but as our nation will have it — if no peace can be made — let us fight like men for our own firesides."

The well-meaning but bewildered Lincoln would have been pained by such comment had it come to his ears. He was, however, too much occupied by crowding events to explain his motives and his plans. Not until the blood and tears of war had cleared men's vision would his patience and his good intentions become clear to his fellow Americans.

The Lincoln call for troops ended the long years of sectional debate. A North and a South, each conscious of its superior ways and each certain of the depravity of the other, now stood ready to give all "in self-defense" and in defense of God's interests.

Lord Charnwood: LINCOLN AND THE WAR

Lincoln has not wanted for defenders among the ranks of historians. Just as each generation has seen critics of Lincoln's pre-war policies, so each generation has found able advocates of his role in the secession crisis. One of the most comprehensive defenses of Lincoln's course of action was written some forty years ago by the gifted British statesman and historian, Lord Charnwood.

WE can best understand the causes which suddenly made [Lincoln] a man of national consequence by a somewhat close examination of the principles and the spirit which governed all his public activity from the moment of the repeal of the Missouri Compromise. The new Republican party which then began to form itself stood for what might seem a simple creed; slavery must be tolerated where it existed because the Constitution and the maintenance of the Union required it, but it must not be allowed to extend beyond its present limits because it was fundamentally wrong. This was what most Whigs and many Democrats in the North had always held, but the formulation of it as the platform of a party, and a party which must draw its members almost entirely from the North, was bound to raise in an acute form questions on which very few men had searched their hearts. Men who hated slavery were likely to falter and find excuses for yielding when confronted with the danger to the Union which would arise. Men who loved the Union might in the last resort be ready to sacrifice it if they could thereby be rid of complicity with slavery, or might be unwilling to maintain it at the cost of fratricidal war.

The stress of conflicting emotions and the complications of the political situation were certain to try to the uttermost the faith of any Republican who was not very sure just how much he cared for the Union and how much for freedom, and what loyalty to either principle involved. It was the distinction of Lincoln — a man lacking in much of the knowledge which statesmen are supposed to possess, and capable of blundering and hesitation about details — first, that upon questions like these he was free from ambiguity of thought or faltering of will, and further, that upon his difficult path, amid bewildering and terrifying circumstances, he was able to take with him the minds of very many very ordinary men.

In a slightly conventional memorial oration upon Clay, Lincoln had said of him that "he loved his country, partly because it was his own country, and mostly because it was a free country." He might truly have said the like of himself. To him the national unity of America, with the Constitution which symbolised it, was the subject of pride and of devotion just in so far as it had embodied and could hereafter more fully embody certain principles of permanent value to mankind. On this he fully knew his own inner mind. For the preservation of an America which he could value more, say, than men value the Argentine Republic, he was to show himself better prepared than any other man to pay any possible price. But he definitely refused to preserve the Union by what in his estimation would have been the real surrender of principles which had made Americans a distinct and self-respecting nation.

Those principles he found in the Declaration of Independence. Its rhetorical inexactitude gave him no trouble, and must not, now that its language is out of fashion, blind us to the fact that the founders of the United States did deliberately aspire to found a commonwealth in which common men and women should count for more than elsewhere, and in which, as we might now phrase it, all authority must defer somewhat to the interests and to the sentiments of the under dog. "Public opinion on any subject," he said, "always has a 'central idea' from which all its minor thoughts radiate. The 'central idea' in our public opinion at the beginning was, and till recently has continued to be, 'the equality of man'; and, although it has always submitted patiently to whatever inequality seemed to be a matter of actual necessity, its constant working has been a steady and progressive effort towards the practical equality of all men." The fathers, he said again, had never intended any such obvious untruth as that equality actually existed, or that any action of theirs could immediately create it; but they had set up a standard to which continual approximation could be made. . . .

But notions of freedom and equality as applied to the negroes presented a real difficulty. "There is," said Lincoln, "a natural disgust in the minds of nearly all white people at the idea of an indiscriminate amalgamation of the white and black men.". . . Lincoln himself disliked the thought of intermarriage between the races. He by no means took it for granted that equality in political power must necessarily and properly follow upon emancipation. Schemes for colonial settlement of the negroes in Africa, or for gradual emancipation accompanied by educational measures, appealed to his sympathy. It was not given him to take a part in the settlement after the war, and it is impossible to guess what he would have achieved as a constructive statesman; but it is certain that he would have proceeded with caution and with the patience of sure faith; and he had that human sympathy with the white people of the South, and no less with the slaves themselves, which taught him the difficulty of the problem. But difficult as the problem was, one solution was certainly wrong, and that was the permanent acquiescence in slavery. If we may judge from reiteration in his speeches, no sophism angered him quite so much as the very popular sophism which defended slavery by presenting a literal equality as the real alternative to it. "I protest against the counterfeit logic which says that since I do not want a negro woman for my slave I must necessarily want her for my wife. I may want her for neither. I may simply let her alone. In some respects she is certainly not my equal. But in her natural right to eat the bread which she has earned by the sweat of her brow, she is my equal and the equal of any man."

The men who had made the Union had, as Lincoln contended, and in regard to most of them contended justly, been true to principle in their dealing with slavery. "They yielded to slavery," he insists, "what the necessity of the case required, and they yielded nothing more." It was, as we know, impossible for them in federating America, however much they might hope to inspire the new nation with just ideas, to take the power of legislating as to slavery within each existing State out of the hands of that State. Such power as they actually possessed of striking at slavery they used, as we have seen and as Lincoln recounted in detail, with all promptitude and almost to its fullest extent. They reasonably believed, though wrongly, that the natural tendency of opinion throughout the now freed Colonies with principles of freedom in the air would work steadily towards emancipation. "The fathers," Lincoln could fairly say, "placed slavery, where the public mind could rest in the belief that it was in the course of ultimate extinction." The task for statesmen now was "to put slavery back where the fathers placed it."

Now this by no means implied that slavery in the States which now adhered to it should be exposed to attack from outside, or the slave owner be denied any right which he could claim under the Constitution, however odious and painful it might be, as in the case of the rendition of fugitive slaves, to yield him his rights. "We allow," says Lincoln, "slavery to exist in the slave States, not because it is right, but from the necessities of the Union. We grant a fugitive slave law because it is so 'nominated in the bond'; because our fathers so stipulated — had to — and we are bound to carry out this agreement." And the obligations to the slave owners and the slave States, which this original agreement and the fundamental necessities of the Union involved, must be fulfilled unswervingly, in spirit as well as in the letter. Lincoln was ready to give the slave States any possible guarantee that the Constitution should not be altered so as to take away

their existing right of self-government in the matter of slavery. He had remained in the past coldly aloof from the Abolitionist propaganda when Herndon and other friends tried to interest him in it, feeling, it seems, that agitation in the free States against laws which existed constitutionally in the slave States was not only futile but improper. With all his power he dissuaded his more impulsive friends from lending any aid to forcible and unlawful proceedings in defence of freedom in Kansas. "The battle of freedom," he exclaims in a vehement plea for what may be called moderate as against radical policy, "is to be fought out on principle. Slavery is violation of eternal right. We have temporised with it from the necessities of our condition; but as sure as God reigns and school children read, that black foul lie can never be consecrated into God's hallowed truth." In other words, the sure way and the only way to combat slavery lay in the firm and the scrupulous assertion of principles which would carry the reason and the conscience of the people with them; the repeal of the prohibition of slavery in the Territories was a defiance of such principles, but so too in its way was the disregard by Abolitionists of the rights covenanted to the slave States. This side of Lincoln's doctrine is apt to jar upon us. We feel with a great American historian that the North would have been depraved indeed if it had not bred Abolitionists, and it requires an effort to sympathise with Lincoln's rigidly correct feeling — sometimes harshly expressed and sometimes apparently cold. It is not possible to us, as it was to him a little later, to look on John Brown's adventure merely as a crime. Nor can we wonder that, when he was President and Civil War was raging, many good men in the North mistook him and thought him half-hearted, because he persisted in his respect for the rights of the Slave States so long as there seemed to be a chance of saving the Union in that way. It was his primary business, he then said, to save the Union if he could; "if I could save the Union by emancipating all the slaves I would do so; if I could save it by emancipating some and not others, I would do that too." But, . . . we shall misread both his policy as President and his character as a man if we fail to see that in the bottom of his mind he felt this forbearance to be required by the very same principles which roused him against the extension of the evil. Years before, he had written to an Abolitionist correspondent that respect for the rights of the slave States was due not only to the Constitution but, "as it seems to me, in a sense to freedom itself." Negro slavery was not the only important issue, nor was it an isolated issue. What really was in issue was the continuance of the nation "dedicated," as he said on a great occasion, "to the proposition that all men are created equal," a nation founded by the Union of self-governing communities, some of which lagged far behind the others in applying in their own midst the elementary principles of freedom, but yet a nation actuated from its very foundation in some important respects by the acknowledgment of human rights.

The practical policy, then, on which his whole efforts were concentrated consisted in this single point — the express recognition of the essential evil of slavery by the enactment that it should not spread further in the Territories subject to the Union. If slavery were thus shut up within a ring fence and marked as a wrong thing which the Union as a whole might tolerate but would not be a party to, emancipation in the slave States

would follow in course of time. It would come about, Lincoln certainly thought, in a way far better for the slaves as well as for their masters, than any forced liberation. He was content to wait for it. "I do not mean that when it takes a turn towards ultimate extinction, it will be in a day, nor in a year, nor in two years. I do not suppose that in the most peaceful way ultimate extinction would occur in less than a hundred years at least, but that it will occur in the best way for both races in God's own good time I have no doubt." If we wonder whether this policy, if soon enough adopted by the Union as a whole, would really have brought on emancipation in the South, the best answer is that, when the policy did receive national sanction by the election of Lincoln, the principal slave States themselves instinctively recognised it as fatal to slavery.

For the extinction of slavery he would wait; for a decision on the principle of slavery he would not. It was idle to protest against agitation of the question. If politicians would be silent that would not get rid of "this same mighty deep-seated power that somehow operates on the minds of men, exciting them and stirring them up in every avenue of society — in politics, in religion, in literature, in morals, in all the manifold relations of life." The stand, temperate as it was, that he advocated against slavery should be taken at once and finally. . . . A definite choice had to be made between the principle of the fathers, which asserted certain rights for all men, and that other principle against which the fathers had rebelled and of which the "divine right of kings" furnished Lincoln with his example. In what particular manner the white people would be made to feel the principle of tyranny when they had definitely "denied freedom to others" and ceased to "deserve it for themselves" Lincoln did not attempt to say, and perhaps only dimly imagined. But he was as convinced as any prophet that America stood at the parting of the ways and must choose now the right principle or the wrong with all its consequences. . . .

It is impossible to estimate how far Lincoln foresaw the strain to which a firm stand against slavery would subject the Union. It is likely enough that those worst forebodings for the Union, which events proved to be very true, were confined to timid men who made a practice of yielding to threats. Lincoln appreciated better than many of his fellows the sentiment of the South, but it is often hard for men, not in immediate contact with a school of thought which seems to them thoroughly perverse, to appreciate its pervasive power, and Lincoln was inclined to stake much upon the hope that reason will prevail. Moreover, he had a confidence in the strength of the Union which might have been justified if his predecessor in office had been a man of ordinary firmness. But it is not to be supposed that any undue hopefulness, if he felt it, influenced his judgment. He was of a temper which does not seek to forecast what the future has to show, and his melancholy prepared him well for any evil that might come. Two things we can say with certainty of his aim and purpose. On the one hand, as has already been said, whatever view he had taken of the peril to the Union he would never have sought to avoid the peril by what appeared to him a surrender of the principle which gave the Union its worth. On the other hand, he must always have been prepared to uphold the Union at whatever the cost might prove to be. To a man of deep and gentle nature war will always be hateful, but it can never, any more than an individual death, appear

the worst of evils. And the claim of the Southern States to separate from a community which to him was venerable and to form a new nation, based on slavery and bound to live in discord with its neighbors, did not appeal to him at all, though in a certain literal sense it was a claim to liberty. His attitude to any possible movement for secession was defined four years at least before secession came, in words such as it was not his habit to use without full sense of their possible effect or without much previous thought. They were quite simple: "We won't break up the Union, and you shan't.". . .

From an early date in November, 1860, every effort was made, by men too numerous to mention, to devise if possible such a settlement of what were now called the grievances of the South as would prevent any other State from following the example of South Carolina. Apart from the intangible difference presented by much disapprobation of slavery in the North and growing resentment in the South as this disapprobation grew louder, the solid ground of dispute concerned the position of slavery in the existing Territories and future acquisitions of the United States Government; the quarrel arose from the election of a President pledged to use whatever power he had, though indeed that might prove little, to prevent the further extension of slavery; and we may almost confine our attention to this point. Other points came into discussion. Several of the Northern States had "Personal Liberty Laws" expressly devised to impede the execution of the Federal law of 1850 as to fugitive slaves. Some attention was devoted to these, especially by Alexander Stephens, who, as the Southern leader most opposed to immediate secession, wished to direct men's minds to a grievance that could be remedied. Lincoln, who had always said that, though the Fugitive Slave Law should be made just and seemly, it ought in substance to be enforced, made clear again that he thought such "Personal Liberty Laws" should be amended, though he protested that it was not for him as President-elect to advise the State Legislatures on their own business. The Republicans generally agreed. Some of the States concerned actually began amending their laws. Thus, if the disquiet of the South had depended on this grievance, the cause of disquiet would no doubt have been removed. Again the Republican leaders, including Lincoln in particular, let there be no ground for thinking that an attack was intended upon slavery in the States where it was established; they offered eventually to give the most solemn pledge possible in this matter by passing an Amendment of the Constitution declaring that it should never be altered so as to take away the independence of the existing slave States as to this portion of their democratic institutions. Lincoln indeed refused on several occasions to make any fresh public disclaimer of an intention to attack existing institutions. His views were "open to all who will read." "For the good men in the South," he writes privately, "— I regard the majority of them as such — I have no objection to repeat them seventy times seven. But I have bad men to deal with both North and South; men who are eager for something new upon which to base new misrepresentations; men who would like to frighten me, or at least fix upon me the character of timidity and cowardice." Nevertheless he endeavoured constantly in private correspondence to narrow and define the issue, which, as he insisted, concerned only the territorial extension of slavery.

The most serious of the negotiations that took place, and to which most hope was attached, consisted in the deliberations of a committee of thirteen appointed by the Senate in December, 1860, which took for its guidance a detailed scheme of compromise put forward by Senator Crittenden, of Kentucky. The efforts of this committee to come to an agreement broke down at the outset upon the question of the Territories, and the responsibility, for good or for evil, of bringing them to an end must probably be attributed to the advice of Lincoln. Crittenden's first proposal was that there should be a Constitutional Amendment declaring that slavery should be prohibited "in all the territory of the United States, now held or hereafter acquired, north of latitude 36°30'" — (the limit fixed in the Missouri Compromise, but restricted then to the Louisiana purchase) — while in all territory, now held or thereafter acquired south of that line, it should be permitted. Crittenden also proposed that when a Territory on either side of the line became a State, it should become free to decide the question for itself; but the discussion never reached this point. On the proposal as to the Territories there seemed at first to be a prospect that the Republicans would agree, in which case the South might very likely have agreed too. The desire for peace was intensely strong among the commercial men of New York and other cities, and it affected the great political managers and the statesmen who, like Seward himself, were in close touch with this commercial influence. Tenacious adherence to declared principle may have been as strong in country districts as the desire for accommodation was in these cities, but it was at any rate far less vocal, and on the whole it seems that compromise was then in the air. It seemed clear from the expressed opinions of his closest allies that Seward would support this compromise. Now Seward just at this time received Lincoln's offer of the office of Secretary of State, a great office and one in which Seward expected to rule Lincoln and the country, but in accepting which, as he did, he made it incumbent on himself not to part company at once with the man who would be nominally his chief. Then there occurred a visit paid on Seward's behalf by his friend Thurlow Weed, an astute political manager but also an able statesman, to Lincoln at Springfield. Weed brought back a written statement of Lincoln's views. Seward's support was not given to the compromise; nor naturally was that of the more radical Republicans, to use a term which now became common; and the Committee of Thirteen found itself unable to agree.

It is unnecessary to repeat what Lincoln's conviction on this, to him the one essential point of policy, was, or to quote from the numerous letters in which from the time of his nomination he tried to keep the minds of his friends firm on this single principle, and to show them that if there were the slightest further yielding as to this, . . . the Southern policy of extending slavery and of "filibustering" against neighbouring counties for that purpose would revive in full force, and the whole labour of the Republican movement would have to begin over again. Since his election he had been writing also to Southern politicians who were personally friendly, to Gilmer of North Carolina, to whom he offered Cabinet office, and to Stephens, making absolutely plain that his difference with them lay in this one point, but making it no less plain that on this point he was, with entire respect to them, immovable. Now, on December 22, the *New York Tribune* was "enabled to state that Mr.

Lincoln stands now as he stood in May last, square upon the Republican platform." The writing that Weed brought to Seward must have said, perhaps more elaborately, the same. If Lincoln had not stood square upon that platform there were others like Senator Wade of Ohio and Senator Grimes of Iowa who might have done so and might have been able to wreck the compromise. Lincoln however, did wreck it, at a time when it seemed likely to succeed, and it is most probable that thereby he caused the Civil War. Probably he avoided making any definite forecast; but he expressed no alarm, and he privately told a friend about this time that "he could not in his heart believe that the South designed the overthrow of the Government." But if he had in his heart believed it, nothing in his life gives reason to think that he would have been more anxious to conciliate the South; on the contrary, it is in line with all we know of his feelings to suppose that he would have thought firmness all the more imperative. We cannot recall the solemnity of his long-considered speech about "a house divided against itself," with which all his word and acts accorded, without seeing that if perhaps he speculated little about the risks, he was prepared to face them whatever they were. Doubtless he took heavy responsibility, but it is painful to find honorable historians, who heartily dislike the cause of slavery, capable to day of wondering whether he was right to do so. "If he had not stood square in December upon the same "platform on which he had stood in May, if he had preferred to enroll himself among those statesmen of all countries whose strongest words are uttered for their own subsequent enjoyment in eating them, he might conceivably have saved much bloodshed, but he would not have left the United States a country of which any good man was proud to be a citizen.

Thus, by the end of 1860, the bottom was really out of the policy of compromise, and it is not worth while to examine the praiseworthy efforts that were still made for it while State after State in the South was deciding to secede. One interesting proposal, which was aired in January, 1861, deserves notice, namely, that the terms of compromise proposed by Crittenden should have been submitted to a vote of the whole people. It was not passed. Seward, whom many people now thought likely to catch at any and every proposal for a settlement, said afterwards with justice that it was "unconstitutional and ineffectual." Ineffectual it would have been in this sense: the compromise would in all probability have been carried by a majority consisting of men in the border States and of all those elsewhere who, though they feared war and desired good feeling, had no further definite opinion upon the chief questions at issue; but it would have left a local majority in many of the Southern States and a local majority in many of the Northern States as irreconcilable with each other as ever. It was opposed also to the spirit of the Constitution. In a great country where the people with infinitely varied interests and opinions can slowly make their predominant wishes appear, but cannot really take counsel together and give a firm decision upon any emergency, there may be exceptional cases when a popular vote on a defined issue would be valuable, significant, desired by the people themselves; but the machinery of representative government, however faulty, is the only machinery by which the people can in some sense govern itself, instead of making itself ungovernable. Above all, in a serious crisis it is supremely repugnant to the spirit of

popular government that the men chosen by a people to govern it should throw their responsibility back at the heads of the electors. It is well to be clear as to the kind of proceeding which the authors of this proposal were really advocating: a statesman has come before the ordinary citizen with a definite statement of the principle on which he would act, and an ordinary citizen has thereupon taken his part in entrusting him with power; then comes the moment for the statesman to carry out his principle, and the latent opposition becomes of necessity more alarming; the statesman is therefore to say to the ordinary citizen, "This is a more difficult matter than I thought; and if I am to act as I said I would, take on yourself the responsibility which I recently put myself forward to bear." The ordinary citizen will naturally as a rule decline a responsibility thus offered him, but he will not be grateful for the offer or glad to be a forced accomplice in this process of indecision.

If we could determine the prevailing sentiment in the North at some particular moment during the crisis, it would probably represent what very few individual men continued to think for six months together. Early in the crisis some strong opponents of slavery were for letting the South go, declaring, as did Horace Greeley of the *New York Tribune*, that "they would not be citizens of a Republic of which one part was pinned to the other part with bayonets". . .

* * *

It is impossible to avoid asking whether . . . this . . . opinion . . . was correct. (The question was indeed an important question in determining the proper course of procedure for a President when confronted with secession.) . . . If we go behind the Constitution, which was then and is now in force, to the original document of which it took the place, we shall find it entitled "Articles of Confederation and Perpetual Union," but we shall not find any such provisions as men desirous of creating a stable and permanent federal government might have been expected to frame. If we read the actual Constitution we shall find no word distinctly implying that a State could or could not secede. As to the real intention of its chief authors, there can be no doubt that they hoped and trusted the Union would prove indissoluble, and equally little doubt that they did not wish to obtrude upon those whom they asked to enter into it the thought that this step would be irrevocable. For the view taken in the South there is one really powerful argument, one which Jefferson Davis insisted passionately in the argumentative memoirs with which he solaced himself in old age. It is that in several of the States, when the Constitution was accepted, public declarations were made to the citizens of those States by their own representatives that a State might withdraw from the Union. But this is far from conclusive. No man gets rid of the obligation of a bond by telling a witness that he does not mean to be bound; the question is not what he means, but what the party with whom he deals must naturally take him to mean. Now the Constitution of the United States upon the face of it purports to create a government able to take its place among the other governments of the world, able if it declares war to wield the whole force of its country in that war, and able if it makes peace to impose that peace upon all its subjects. This seems to imply that the authority of that government over part of the country should be legally indefeasible. It would have been ridiculous

if, during a war with Great Britain, States on the Canadian border should have had the legal right to secede, and set up a neutral government with a view to subsequent reunion with Great Britain. The sound legal view of this matter would seem to be: that the doctrine of secession is so repugnant to the primary intention with which the national instrument of government was framed that it could only have been supported by an express reservation of the right to secede in the Constitution itself.

The Duke of Argyll, one of the few British statesmen of the time who followed this struggle with intelligent interest, briefly summed up the question thus: "I know of no government in the world that could possibly have admitted the right of secession from its own allegiance.". . .

But to say — as in a legal sense we may — that the Southern States rebelled is not necessarily to say that they were wrong. . . . It sometimes seems to be held that when a decided majority of the people whose voices can be heard, in a more or less defined area, elect to live for the future under a particular government, all enlightened men elsewhere would wish them to have their way. If any such principle could be accepted without qualification, few movements for independence would ever have been more completely justified than the secession of the Southern States. If we set aside the highland region of which mention has already been made, in the six cotton-growing States which first seceded, and in several of those which followed as soon as it was clear that secession would be resisted, the preponderance of opinion in favour of the movement was overwhelming. This was not only so among the educated and governing portions of society, which were interested in slav ery. While the negroes themselves were unorganised and dumb and made no stir for freedom, the poorer class of white people, to whom the institution of slavery was in reality oppressive, were quite unconscious of this; the enslavement of the negro appeared to them a tribute to their own dignity, and their indiscriminating spirit of independence responded enthusiastically to the appeal that they should assert themselves against the real or fancied pretensions of the North. . . . [B]roadly speaking, it is certain that the movement for secession was begun with at least as general an enthusiasm and maintained with at least as loyal a devotion as any national movement with which it can be compared.

The deliberate endeavor of a people to separate themselves from the political sovereignty under which they live and set up a new political community, in which their national life shall develop itself more fully or more securely, must always command a certain respect. Whether it is entitled further to the full sympathy and to the support or at least acquiescence of others is a question which in particular cases involves considerations such as cannot be foreseen in any abstract discussion of political theory. But, speaking very generally, it is a question in the main of the worth which we attribute on the one hand to the common life to which it is sought to give freer scope, and on the other hand to the common life which may thereby be weakened or broken up. . . .

. . . If the slave States had been suffered to depart in peace they would have set up a new and peculiar political society, more truly held together than the original Union by a single avowed principle; a nation dedicated to the inequality of men. It is not really possible to think of the free national life which they could thus have initiated as a thing to be respected and preserved. Nor is it true that their choice for themselves of this dingy freedom was no concern of their neighbours. We have seen how the slave interest hankered for enlarged dominion; and it is certain that the Southern Confederacy, once firmly established, would have been an aggressive and disturbing power upon the continent of America. The questions of territorial and other rights between it and the old Union might have been capable of satisfactory settlement for the moment, or they might have proved as insoluble as Lincoln thought they were. But, at the best, if the States which adhered to the old Union had admitted the claim of the first seceding States to go, they could only have retained for themselves an insecure existence as a nation, threatened at each fresh conflict of interest or sentiment with a further disruption which could not upon any principle have been resisted. . . .

. . . Observers at the time and historians after are easily mistaken as to popular feeling; the acute fluctuations of opinion inevitable among journalists, and in any sort of circle where men are constantly meeting and talking politics, may leave the great mass of quiet folk almost unaffected. We may be sure that there was a considerable body of steady opinion very much in accord with Lincoln; this should not be forgotten, but it must not be supposed that it prevailed constantly. On the contrary, it was inherent in the nature of the crisis that opinion wavered and swayed. We should miss the whole significance of Lincoln's story if we did not think of the North now and to the end of the war as exposed to disunion, hesitation, and quick reaction. If at this time a sufficiently authoritative leader with sufficiently determined timidity had inaugurated a policy of stampede, he might have had a vast and tumultuous following. Only his following would quickly, if too late, have repented. What was wanted, if the people of the North were to have what most justly might be called their way, was a leader who would not seem to hurry them along, nor yet be ever looking round to see if they followed, but just go groping forward among the innumerable obstacles, guided by such principles of good sense and of right as would perhaps on the whole and in the long run be approved by the maturer thought of most men; and Lincoln was such a leader. . . .

Avery Craven: THE CIVIL WAR: A BREAKDOWN OF THE DEMOCRATIC PROCESS

Avery Craven's recent writings have dealt with the significance of the Civil War in the nation's history. Craven's general view is that the war marked a breakdown of the democratic process of rational discussion of issues and compromise of differences. He believes that war came largely because concrete problems were reduced to the level of abstract values where men fight and die rather than resolve their differences through the normal institutions of political democracy.

I*

THE Civil War is the most significant event in the domestic history of the United States. It marks the dividing line between an old order and Modern America. It eliminated the South as an important factor in shaping national policies and ended the domination of rural groups in American life. It opened the way for modern industrial and finance capitalism. It put the major control of national affairs into the keeping of the urban dwellers of the Northeast. It was, indeed, what Charles A. Beard has called it — "The Second American Revolution."

And the significant thing about the American Civil War is that it represents a complete breakdown of the democratic process in the handling of national problems. Men ceased to reason together. Discussion of issues turned to incrimination; compromise or delay in action became impossible. Men firm in the conviction that the totality of right and justice was on their side faced each other with a willingness and a determination to use violence for the achievement of their ends. In the end, opponents were beaten into submission in bloody combat in complete contradiction of the basic assumption on which the whole American political structure had been erected, namely, that men are endowed with reason enough to rule themselves and that they have consciences which impel them to deal justly with their fellows; that rational discussion of issues, compromise of differences, and delay in action where adjustment is not reached, constitute a procedure by which groups that vary as much as the colony of Massachusetts and the colony of South Carolina had varied could live and work in unity forever.

For these reasons the Civil War continues to be a matter of vital interest to all historians of the United States, and one about which there has been less agreement than about any other event in the history of the nation. Historians are far apart in their interpretations and, strangely enough, in a field so compli-

* Excerpted from Avery Craven, "The Civil War and the Democratic Process," *The Abraham Lincoln Quarterly*, IV (June, 1947), 269–287, 290. Reprinted by permission.

cated that any honest effort to throw light into darkness should be welcomed, there has been little of cooperation and much of name-calling, distortion of positions, and open charges of bias. The passions of 1860–1865 seem still to exist, especially among those who have done little research in the vast materials on both sides, and the hope for a better understanding of America's greatest tragedy is yet a long way off.

It is not my purpose today to attempt any full discussion of events and factors that entered into the making of a Civil War in the United States. I only wish to suggest to you certain approaches to the matter of the breakdown of the democratic process in 1860, which may have some permanent value to those who still retain their faith in that process as the best way for humble men to govern themselves.

I would begin with two great American documents and their differences in emphasis — the Declaration of Independence and the Constitution of the United States. I would like to suggest a dilemma inherent in their implications and in their significance in American life.

When the Continental Congress, on July 2, 1776, had passed the Virginia Resolutions officially declaring our independence of Great Britain, they thought it necessary to justify the step they had taken. So they appointed a committee, of which Thomas Jefferson was a member, to make such a statement. It presented, on July 4, 1776, a document that has ever since been known as The Declaration of Independence.

That document contained two things: a political philosophy justifying rebellion and a statement of the grievances of the colonies against the British king.

The statement of grievances was a rather labored affair not always exactly sound from an historical point of view and, strangely enough, completely ignoring the British parliament against whose acts and encroachments they had for years been complaining. It served their purposes, however, and has since been largely ignored even by scholars who are seeking the facts as to the causes of the American Revolution.

The ringing phrases of the political philosophy, on the other hand, quickly became a part of the American heritage, a weapon to be used against tyranny of every kind, a constant prod toward making American practices coincide with American ideals:

We hold these truths to be self-evident, That all men are created equal, that they are endowed by their Creator with certain unalienable rights; that among these are life, liberty, and the pursuit of happiness; that to secure these rights, governments are instituted among men, deriving their just powers from the consent of the governed; that whenever any form of government becomes destructive of these ends, it is the right of the people to alter or to abolish it, and to institute new government, laying its foundation on such principles, and organizing its powers in such form, as to them shall seem most likely to effect their safety and happiness.

The ideas here expressed were not new. They were a part of the Natural Rights philosophy, used first to justify rebellion against the English king in 1688, and widely current in the eighteenth century when the works of Isaac Newton became generally known. With Newton, as you remember, God had withdrawn from the immediate and direct manipulation of the universe and had left it to be run by laws which gave order and security. By his intelligence man could know these laws; by conformity he could avoid disaster and turn them to his benefit. And God as the creator of man had also created a moral law for man's government, and had endowed man with reason by which to comprehend it, and a conscience that created the obligation to obedience. "Underneath and supporting human society, as the basic rock supports the hills, was a moral order which was the abiding place of the eternal principles of truth and righteousness."

That meant that there was a right and a wrong in social things; that there was a good society and a bad society; that the laws and institutions of man should approximate the moral law and the moral order. If they fell short then there was the "higher law," and "civil disobedience" became a virtue. Social conduct was thus a matter of conscience rather than obedience to existing law. Social justice was an obligation, and the existence of conditions which reason and conscience condemned was a matter for concern and action. The fight for social justice became a part of "the eternal struggle between right and wrong." Politics and Christianity had common ends. To secure the equality of all men; to guarantee to them life, liberty and the pursuit of happiness, was a moral obligation. And all just men, through reason and conscience, knew exactly what each of these things meant.

Out of Revolutionary thinking and the trends of the age came a second document, the Constitution of the United States. In resisting England and the acts of the British parliament, the colonists assumed that they had certain rights which belonged to them as Englishmen. They believed that there was a great body of English precedent, a set of British documents, which guaranteed to Englishmen everywhere and at all times, certain rights and the protection of certain interests. Some spoke as though these formed a British constitution, and as though this constitution was a bulwark against oppression and injustice — that it permanently fixed relations within the empire.

So when they had declared their independence, they followed a growing practice of the age and put down in written form a description of their common government and its rights and limitations. When this proved inadequate they formed "a more perfect Union" and established "this Constitution for the United States of America." Here they described the machinery and functioning of government and the distribution of powers between its agents; listed the powers of the central and the state governments. As completed it revealed a government of checks and balances that was to be altered only by prescribed methods. It too, when amended with a Bill of Rights, was to be a bulwark against aggression, a shelter behind which both men and states and their rights would be secure.

And since the Fathers who framed the Constitution were just men — men who gave full play to reason and conscience, it could be assumed that the grants and restrictions placed in the Constitution aimed at a good society and at the approximation of the moral order that all Americans accepted.

Now here were two fundamental American documents, — the one framed to *establish* a government; the other framed to *justify revolution* against a government. The one intended to set up a more perfect Union and protect the fixed rights of men against the whims and passions of those who might destroy; the other intended to stress those abstract rights of mankind which grow and expand and change almost constantly —

rights of human beings ultimately resting on the "higher law" that knows no fixed bounds save those of a just and moral universe.

As a pure abstraction such differences were of no consequence, but what if some fine day one group of Americans should appeal to one of these documents to prove and protect *its* rights and interests, and another group of Americans should appeal to the other document to prove and protect a conflicting set of rights and interests? What if the law of the land as embodied in the Constitution should not remain in accord with some men's reason and conscience, and they should appeal to the Declaration of Independence and the higher laws it justifies? Then, perhaps, the Constitution would be burned and the phrases of the Declaration would be dismissed as mere "glittering generalities" — as doctrine, both "false and foolish."

That, I judge, would constitute a conflict of basic values, of moral standards; of the most fundamental things in the national make-up, and create a situation where discussion would be utterly useless and compromise impossible.

The second situation that I would notice was the heavy strain placed on the American political structure by the rapid growth and expansion of the period from 1830 to 1860. These years, the life span of a single generation, saw population increase nearly two and a half times and spread, with gaps on the plains and in the mountain regions, to the Pacific coast. A great Southwestern kingdom was added by the annexation of Texas and by conquest from Mexico. The industrial revolution reached maturity in the Northeast, and New York City, Boston, and Philadelphia became centers of commerce and finance national and international in scope. Agriculture more

than kept pace. In the Northwest the kingdom of wheat, and, in the Southwest, the kingdom of cotton, poured out surpluses capable of caring for the needs of both Europe and America. Steam applied to transportation on land and on water shrunk space by halves and thirds, and altered all the concepts of distance held by the generation that framed the Constitution.

Growth and expansion produced two conflicting results which bear directly on the problem we are considering. Developments of different kinds in different parts of the nation tended to exaggerate sectional interests and attitudes. Regions already distinct in character and needs became more so under augmenting forces. Sectional consciousness increased and sectional rivalry became more intense. Westward expansion increased the demand for more liberal land legislation and for government aid in building internal improvements along which western produce could move to market. Opposition by South and East to such measures stirred deep resentment and bitter words. The growth of industry brought quick demands for protective tariffs from men of the Northeast, and the spread of cotton across the South brought equally strong demands for free trade. Banking and commercial interests in the North found need for a stronger central government; the planting interests with slave labor turned more and more toward the state for security and approval. Men began to talk about civilizations based on "peculiar" interests and values that were rising in different corners of the nation.

But that was only one side of developments. The *facts* of *increased interdependence* and growing *national interest* were even more important. Vastly more significant than sectionalism was the fact that the United States was becoming a *great nation* among the nations of the earth. By 1860 its population had passed that of the United Kingdom and was rapidly closing the gap on France and Germany. Foreign immigrants, who knew nothing of sections, were pouring into the country; floods of native Americans swept westward across state line after state line in answer to the call of gold or fertile soils. Where in earlier days foreign commerce dominated, now internal trade came to the fore to signify "the transition from colonial to national economy." That meant sectional interdependence. The South, with its heavy concentration on staple crops, formed a splendid market for the horses, mules, tobacco, bagging, and surplus slaves of the border states, the foodstuffs of the Northwest, and the manufactures of the Northeast. It provided opportunities to the ships and shippers of the North and to the bankers of Eastern cities who often financed both the production and the marketing of Southern crops. Its cotton, in turn, kept Northeastern factories busy and its rice and sugar added to the nation's food supply. The Northwest, as an expanding frontier, needed manufactured goods, as well as financial assistance in the purchase of lands and the building of internal improvements which could be secured only from the Northeast and from Europe. The Northeast needed raw materials for its factories, and food for its dependent urban workers, which could come only from South and West. And thus the packet, the steamship and the railroad shuttled back and forth between supply and demand to weave the pattern of a national economy and to demonstrate the interdependence of life in the modern world.

Nor had Americans been unconscious of the significance of these developments nor lacking in national pride because of them. It showed itself in the swaggering demands for territorial expansion that passed under the guise of "Manifest Destiny"; in the sharp reaction against foreign immigrants who might ruin the great experiment in democracy; in the strident efforts of "Young America" to intervene in behalf of battling European liberals; in the quick emergence of a native literature that began its statement by insisting that: "Our day of dependence, our long apprenticeship to other lands, draws to a close. . . . We will walk on our own feet; we will work with our own hands; we will speak our own minds."

Other peoples also felt the force of the new national consciousness. Our dealings with Mexico were brusque enough to produce war and the open charge of aggression from half the nation itself. Great Britain bristled at Polk's bumptious diplomacy and then good-naturedly yielded to compromise. Spain, less graciously, accepted disavowal of swashbuckling efforts to force her to yield Cuba; and the sullen Indians retreated step by step in front of settlers bearing letters of marque from God.

The strain on the political structure produced by sectional growth and rivalry was, indeed, great. The question of national policy in regard to lands, internal improvements, tariffs, the bank, and expansion, all brought bitter strife in Congress and, on one occasion, a move by South Carolina for nullification. Every man who aspired to national leadership had to voice the demands of his own section in regard to each of these issues and, at the same time, shape his appeal in such a way as to win support in other sections or at least to soften opposition. Most programs offered had a double purpose or appeal. Calhoun's land cession bills were framed both to win Western support, by land and internal improvement aid, and to prevent an increase of tariff rates. Clay's American system offered tariffs to industrial areas and internal improvements to the needy agricultural belts. His bills for the distribution of the proceeds from public land sales were intended not only to settle the land question but also to deplete the public treasury and thereby justify tariff increases. Benton linked pre-emption and graduation together in order to please both the older and newer public land areas, and Webster frankly stressed the national appeal in order to weaken opposing combinations that threatened New England tariffs.

Yet, in spite of all differences and all individual maneuvering, one agent stood out above all others to weaken local loyalties and to bind divergent geographic elements into national unity. That was the national political party. Whether Whig or Democrat, Americans manifested the most ardent devotion to party and the most intense feelings against party rivals. For party's sake men were willing to sacrifice sectional interest and to yield even personal principles. The very fact of membership in a party and allegiance to its platform was a personal compromise and the party, as such, could yield where individuals could not. Men with consciences could belong to parties that had none. And party loyalty, reaching beyond all local borders, worked steadily for sectional agreement and for national compromise.

Political parties, nevertheless, felt the strain of sectional strife and alternated control of the national government from 1836 to 1856. No party could succeed itself and no president could secure a second term. No important party leader reached the presidency, and dark horses and figurehead candidates were put forward in every election.

The strain was heavy; yet the strong national undercurrent held the parties together and prevented either Democrats or Whigs from assuming a strictly sectional character. The level of debate in Congress was high, and workable compromises or adjustments were reached on lands, tariffs, internal improvements, and even finances. A successful foreign war was fought, with considerable opposition it is true, but with all the bipartisan support necessary. The democratic process was functioning well. Policies were being established and issues adjusted. The nation was moving steadily forward to maturity and strength. The experiment in democratic government, at least up to 1848, seemed to be succeeding. It was, however, a purely political success — one which accepted the claims of sectionalism and established ways as equal to those of a crowding, driving modern nationalism with its new technologies and social interdependence.

Historians generally agree that the complete breakdown and ultimate abandonment of that process in the next thirteen years was due to the institution of slavery. To read some of their writings one would think that "the dark cloud of slavery" appeared suddenly out of nowhere in the years around 1850; that, for the first time men had become conscious of its evils and launched a great moral crusade against an institution that had no place in the modern world. As a matter of fact the whole situation had existed for over two hundred years. Slavery in the United States just before the Civil War was most certainly a more humane affair than it had been in earlier times. Nor had it lacked critics. All through the years some men had complained of its injustice, its evil effects on both master and slave, and its violation of every ideal held by both democrats and Christians. As late as 1832 members of the Virginia House of Delegates had denounced the holding "of any part of the human race in bondage" as an act "of injustice, tyranny, and oppression." They had pointed out its baneful effects on both blacks and whites; they had called it a "transcendent evil . . . a mildew which has blighted in its course every region it has touched, from the creation of the world . . ."; they had ascribed the backward condition of agriculture and industry in Virginia to its presence; and had insisted that the day when men would listen to its defense with patience or forbearance, had gone forever.

The historian's problem is, therefore, *not* whether slavery was a great evil, or whether there was just at this time a sharp moral reaction against it which had a major part in producing the Civil War. Both those things can be taken for granted, and let me say once and for all that I know of no historian who has ever questioned either of them. The real problem is how did the slavery issue happen to take the form it did take in these years, and why did it produce the effects it did produce.

In the first place the opposition to slavery which brought the final break was not opposition to slavery per se or even opposition to slavery in the states where it existed. It was simply opposition to *the extension of slavery*. It was being carried on, not by anti-slavery societies, but by politicians and political parties. The abolitionist was still at work even though his organizations had split and weakened, but the men who led the new and fatal drive against slavery, had almost as little use for the abolitionist as did the slaveholder, himself. . . .

This is not to say that these men did not think slavery wrong. They most certainly did, and they said so! It was a moral issue, but their determination not to see it spread to the territories had back of it something more in their firm belief in the capacity of a free democratic society to produce an ideal economic and social order. Slavery was a blight. Southern life was backward. Slaves were wasteful; Southern fields were tumbledown; the South was out of step with progress. Freedom alone would give the greatest prosperity, and alone permit advancement toward that social-economic millennium which was being realized in these free United States. They linked the growth of industry and commerce and agriculture with a free democratic order. They believed that they were achieving something of the perfect society made possible by the laws of nature and nature's God. The very growth of Northern and Western population, the rise of Northern cities, Northern commerce, and Northern industry, all demonstrated the value of freedom and the fact that these people were in step with the nation's true destiny.

That what was evolving was finance and industrial capitalism did not matter just then. The problem was one of checking slavery as the great enemy of democratic progress. That was as much a moral job as was the destruction of slavery itself.

In addition to this, there had grown up, since Polk's election in 1844, a strong belief that the Democratic party was becoming the party of slavery. Texas was annexed, but the Oregon boundary was not pushed to 54°40'. The Walker tariff moved sharply towards free trade, and a river and harbor bill met the president's veto on constitutional grounds. Homestead legislation seemed further off than ever. For the first time Northern men talked of "the slave-power" and linked the policies of government with its influence. The Wilmot Proviso, which they devised to check slavery's advantage in lands acquired from Mexico, was their answer. Back of it was not only a determination to check the spread of slavery, but also an equal determination to check the "slave power." And that, more and more, meant checking the Democratic party. As Wyndham Robertson complainingly put it: "The possession of the power of the Federal Government by the Democratic party . . . furnished the pretext . . . to confound the whole slaveholding interest as absolutely identical with Democracy, and thus to turn and direct opposition, for whatever cause, to the policy and acts of the Democratic party, into apparent opposition to the slaveholding interests." "This ruse," he charged, "fused . . . and united into a common line of policy, some who merely opposed the administration on political grounds, with its opponents on the slavery issue."

This belief in the Democratic party as the agent of "the slave power" reached a climax, when Stephen A. Douglas introduced his Kansas-Nebraska Bill. The "Appeal of the Independent Democrats" which Chase and his fellows issued was a call to revolt. The formation of the Republican party which followed was the political answer to a political situation in which, as they believed, slavery dominated the Democratic party. The combination of opposition to the extension of slavery and such material things as tariffs, railways to the Pacific, river and harbor improvements, homesteads and encouragement of immigration in the Republican program was natural and necessary. The purpose and end of both

was one and the same — freedom and progress!

But there was more in the way than the Democratic party. Increasingly it was apparent that the Constitution of the United States was being used to check Northern demands and to protect slave interests. First it had been the tariff which South Carolina had attempted to check on grounds of unconstitutionality. Then Polk had rejected the much needed river and harbor bill on constitutional grounds, and Pierce had followed the precedent. In the territorial struggle Southerners had insisted both on the constitutional obligation of Congress to protect slavery in the territories and on the unconstitutionality of Congressional interference with slavery in the territories. The courts had aided by declaring the Missouri Compromise unconstitutional and had repeatedly upheld the rights of masters to recover their fugitive slaves.

Through Southern statements of the period ran the word "Constitution" like the repeated call of a whip-poor-will. "We invoke the spirit of the Constitution, and claim its guarantees," said the resolutions of the Nashville Convention. "We will stand by the right; we will take the Constitution; we will defend it by the sword with the halter around our necks," avowed Robert Toombs in the Senate. ". . . The South should never yield one atom of her full, just, and *equal* rights under the Constitution," wrote H. L. Berguin. "If it be true . . . that there is a large majority of the people of the North who are unwilling to stand by the constitutional guarantees," spoke Alexander H. Stephens, "I, for one, am for tearing asunder every bond that binds us together. . . . Any people capable of defending themselves, who would continue their allegiance to a government which should deny them a clear, unquestionable, constitutional right of the magnitude and importance of this to the people of the South, would deserve to be stigmatized as poltroons." And when steps to disunion were already under way it was Stephens again who pleaded with the people, saying: ". . . We are pledged to maintain the Constitution. . . . If all our hopes are to be blasted, if the Republic is to go down, let us be found to the last moment standing on the deck with the Constitution of the United States waving over our heads. Let the fanatics of the North break the Constitution, if such is their fell purpose. Let the responsibility be upon them. . . ."

To meet such appeal to rights under the Constitution there were only two methods. First, the Constitution could be burned. That Garrison and his friends adopted. The second method was to turn to that other equally good American document, The Declaration of Independence. That the Republicans did. . . .

Seward early declared: ". . . I know that there are laws of various sorts which regulate the conduct of men. There are constitutions and statutes, codes mercantile and codes civil; but when we are legislating for states, especially when we are founding states, all these laws must be brought to the standard of the laws of God, and must be tried by that standard, and must stand or fall by it." Later he declared that ". . . The abstractions of human rights are the only permanent foundations of society. It is by referring to them that men determine what is established because it is RIGHT, in order to uphold it forever; and what is right only because it is established, in order that they may lawfully change it, in accordance with the increase of knowledge and the progress of reason."

To Seward slavery was clearly one of the things that "the increase of knowledge and the progress of reason" had left back in the "Dark Ages." He was certain that "we cannot, in our judgment, be either true Christians or real freemen, if we impose on another a chain that we defy all human power to fasten on ourselves." And if some defended it because it was "established" by the Constitution, then there was "a higher law than the Constitution," which, in the case of slavery in the territories, devoted them "to union, to justice, to defence, to welfare, and to liberty," as a part "of the common heritage of mankind, bestowed upon them by the Creator of the universe.". . .

Abraham Lincoln's own final judgment regarding the sectional conflict was that it was part of "the eternal conflict between right and wrong." On his way to assume the presidency he declared that the great principle or idea that had kept this confederacy together was "not the mere matter of the separation of the Colonies from the mother land; but that sentiment in the Declaration of Independence which gave liberty, not alone to the people of this country, but, I hope, to the world for all future time. It was that which gave promise that in due time the weight would be lifted from the shoulders of all men. This is a sentiment embodied in the Declaration of Independence. . . ." And in his first message to Congress he insisted that the whole struggle was "for maintaining in the world that form and substance of government whose leading object is to elevate the condition of men; to lift artificial weights from all shoulders; to clear the paths of laudable pursuit for all; to afford all an unfettered start and a fair chance in the race of life."

No wonder he hailed Thomas Jefferson as the man "who, in the concrete pressure of a struggle for national independence by a single people, had the coolness, forecast, and capacity to introduce into a merely revolutionary document, an abstract truth, applicable to all men and all times, and so to embalm it there, that to-day, and in all coming days, it shall be a rebuke and a stumbling-block to the very harbingers of re-appearing tyranny and oppression."

The full implication of a genuine acceptance of the doctrines of the Declaration of Independence and the moral law which it carried, was not fully understood even by those who professed it. Seward did say bluntly that "slavery and freedom are conflicting systems, brought together by the union of the states, not neutralized, nor even harmonized," and that though "you may slay the Wilmot Proviso in the Senate chamber, and bury it beneath the capitol today; the dead corse, in complete steel, will haunt your legislative halls tomorrow," yet he did not believe the Union in danger. Lincoln, in turn, talked of "a house divided against itself," that could not stand, yet he did not believe that it would fall. Both attempted while they preached the revolutionary doctrines of the Declaration, to retain respect for the Constitution *as they interpreted it.* They, of course, had to reject the Supreme Court's interpretation of the Constitution and good Republicans even talked of reconstructing the Court so as to secure the kind of decisions they wanted. Yet some men more logically and boldly said: "The fact that a law is constitutional amounts to nothing, unless it is also pure; it must harmonize with the law of God, or be set at nought by all upright men.". . .

Such attitudes, if confined to idealistic reformers, would not have wrecked a nation. When held by politicians and made a part of party politics, they meant the end of national parties and the building up of sectional parties pledged to action. . . .

II*

The matter of how issues got beyond the abilities of the democratic process. . . has to do with the way in which concrete issues were reduced to abstract principles and the conflicts between interests simplified to basic levels where men feel more than they reason and where compromise or yielding is impossible because issues appear in the form of right or wrong and involve the fundamental structure of society. This is not saying, as some have charged, that great moral issues were not involved. They certainly were, and it is a matter of choice with historians as to whether or not they take sides, praise or condemn, become partisans in this departed quarrel, or use past events for present-day purposes.

As an approach to this . . . problem, a correspondence which took place between Abraham Lincoln and Alexander H. Stephens between November 30 and December 22, 1860, is highly revealing. On November 14, Stephens had delivered one of the great speeches of his life before the legislature of Georgia. It was a Union speech. He had begged his fellow Southerners not to give up the ship, to wait for some violation of the Constitution before they attempted secession. Equality might yet be possible inside the Union. At least, the will of the whole people should be obtained before any action was taken.

Abraham Lincoln, still unconvinced that there was real danger, wrote Stephens, as an old friend, for a revised copy of his speech. Stephens complied, and he ended his letter with a warning

---

* Excerpted from Avery Craven, "The 1840s and the Democratic Process," *Journal of Southern History*, XVI (May, 1950), 162–164. Reprinted by permission.

about the great peril which threatened the country and a reminder of the heavy responsibility now resting on the president-elect's shoulders. Lincoln answered with assurance that he would not *"directly,* or *indirectly,* interfere with the slaves" or with the southern people about their slaves, and then closed with this significant statement: "I suppose, however, this does not meet the case. You think slavery is right and ought to be extended, while we think it is *wrong* and ought to be restricted. That I suppose is the rub. It certainly is the only substantial difference between us."

The reduction of "the only substantial difference" between North and South to a simple question of *right and wrong* is the important thing about Lincoln's statement. It revealed the extent to which the sectional controversy had, by 1860, been simplified and reduced to a conflict of principles in the minds of the northern people.

Stephens' answer to Lincoln's letter is equally revealing. He expressed "an earnest desire to preserve and maintain the Union of the States, if it can be done upon the principles and in furtherance of the objects for which it was formed." He insisted, however, that private opinion on the question of "African Slavery" was not a matter over which "the Government under the Constitution" had any control. "But now," he said, "this subject which is confessedly on all sides outside of the Constitutional action of the Government so far as the States are concerned, is made the 'central idea' in the Platform of principles announced by the triumphant party." It was this total disregard of the Constitution and the rights guaranteed under it that lay back of southern fears. It was the introduction into party politics of issues which projected action by Congress outside its constitutional powers that had made all the trouble. Stephens used the word "Constitution" seven times in his letter.

The significant thing here is Stephens' reduction of sectional differences to the simple matter of southern rights under the Constitution. He too showed how completely the sectional controversy had been simplified into a conflict of principles. And he with Lincoln, speaking for the North and South, emphasized the fact that after years of strife the complex issues between the sections had assumed the form of a conflict between *right* and *rights.*

To the scholar it must be perfectly clear that this drastic simplification of sectional differences did not mean that either Lincoln or Stephens thought that all the bitter economic, social, and political questions could be ignored. It simply meant that right and rights had become the symbols or carriers of all those interests and values. Yet it is equally clear that as symbols they carried an emotional force and moral power in themselves that was far greater than the sum total of all the material issues involved. They suggested things which cannot be compromised — things for which men willingly fight and die.

Arthur Schlesinger, Jr.: THE CIVIL WAR: A CRISIS OF MORAL DECISION

Arthur Schlesinger, Jr., is one of the most celebrated of contemporary historians. The youngest historian to receive the Pulitzer prize, Schlesinger has also received the Bancroft award and other citations for his distinguished studies in the political and intellectual history of the United States. Although not primarily a student of the Civil War period, Schlesinger's writings have had an important influence on historical thought on the subject. This selection states the view that the position of the South on the Slavery question presented Northern leaders with a moral crisis which could be resolved only through war.

THE Civil War was our great national trauma. A savage fraternal conflict, it released deep sentiments of guilt and remorse — sentiments which have reverberated through our history and our literature ever since. Literature in the end came to terms with these sentiments by yielding to the South in fantasy the victory it had been denied in fact; this tendency culminated on the popular level in *Gone with the Wind* and on the highbrow level in the Nashville cult of agrarianism. But history, a less malleable medium, was constricted by the intractable fact that the war had taken place, and by the related assumption that it was, in William H. Seward's phrase, an "irrepressible conflict," and hence a justified one.

As short a time ago as 1937, for example, even Professor James G. Randall could describe himself as "unprepared to go to the point of denying that the great American tragedy could have been avoided." Yet in a few years the writing of history would succumb to the psychological imperatives which had produced *I'll Take my Stand* and *Gone with the Wind;* and Professor Randall would emerge as the leader of a triumphant new school of self-styled "revisionists." The publication of two vigorous books by Professor Avery Craven — *The Repressible Conflict* (1939) and *The Coming of the Civil War* (1942) — and the appearance of Professor Randall's own notable volumes on Lincoln — *Lincoln the President: Springfield to Gettysburg* (1945), *Lincoln and the South* (1946), and *Lincoln the Liberal Statesman* (1947) — brought about a profound reversal of the professional historian's attitude toward the Civil War. Scholars now denied the traditional assumption of the inevitability of the war and boldly advanced the thesis that a "blundering generation" had transformed a "repressible conflict" into a "needless war."

Arthur Schlesinger, Jr., "The Causes of the Civil War: A Note on Historical Sentimentalism," *Partisan Review*, XVI (Oct., 1949), 969–981. Reprinted with permission.

The swift triumph of revisionism came about with very little resistance or even expressed reservations on the part of the profession. Indeed, the only adequate evaluation of the revisionist thesis that I know was made, not by an academic historian at all, but by that illustrious semi-pro, Mr. Bernard De Voto; and Mr. De Voto's two brilliant articles in *Harper's* in 1945 unfortunately had little influence within the guild. By 1947 Professor Allan Nevins, summing up the most recent scholarship in *Ordeal of the Union,* his able general history of the eighteen-fifties, could define the basic problem of the period in terms which indicated a measured but entire acceptance of revisionism. "The primary task of statesmanship in this era," Nevins wrote, "was to furnish a workable adjustment between the two sections, while offering strong inducements to the southern people to regard their labor system not as static but evolutionary, and equal persuasions to the northern people to assume a helpful rather than scolding attitude."

This new interpretation surely deserves at least as meticulous an examination as Professor Randall is prepared to give, for example, to such a question as whether or not Lincoln was playing fives when he received the news of his nomination in 1860. The following notes are presented in the interests of stimulating such an examination.

The revisionist case, as expounded by Professors Randall and Craven, has three main premises. First:

(1) that the Civil War was caused by the irresponsible emotionalization of politics far out of proportion to the real problems involved. The war, as Randall put it, was certainly not caused by cultural variations nor by economic rivalries nor by sectional differences; these all existed, but it was "stupid," as he declared,

to think that they required war as a solution. "One of the most colossal of misconceptions" was the "theory" that "fundamental motives produce war. The glaring and obvious fact is the artificiality of war-making agitation." After all, Randall pointed out, agrarian and industrial interests had been in conflict under Coolidge and Hoover; yet no war resulted. "In Illinois," he added, "major controversies (not mere transient differences) between downstate and metropolis have stopped short of war."

Nor was the slavery the cause. The issues arising over slavery were in Randall's judgment "highly artificial, almost fabricated. . . . They produced quarrels out of things that would have settled themselves were it not for political agitation." Slavery, Craven observed, was in any case a much overrated problem. It is "perfectly clear," he wrote, "that slavery played a rather minor part in the life of the South and of the Negro."

What then was the cause of war? "If one word or phrase were selected to account for war," wrote Randall, ". . . it would have to be such a word as fanaticism (on both sides), misunderstanding, misrepresentation, or perhaps politics." Phrases like "whipped-up crisis" and "psychopathic case" adorned Randall's explanation. Craven similarly described the growing sense of sectional differences as "an artificial creation of inflamed minds." The "molders of public opinion steadily created the fiction of two distinct peoples." As a result, "distortion led a people into bloody war."

If uncontrolled emotionalism and fanaticism caused the war, how did they get out of hand? Who whipped up the "whipped-up crisis"? Thus the second revisionist thesis:

(2) that sectional friction was permitted to develop into needless war by

the inexcusable failure of political leadership in the fifties. "It is difficult to achieve a full realization of how Lincoln's generation stumbled into a ghastly war," wrote Randall. ". . . If one questions the term 'blundering generation,' let him inquire how many measures of the time he would wish copied or repeated if the period were to be approached with a clean slate and to be lived again."

It was the politicians, charged Craven, who systematically sacrificed peace to their pursuit of power. Calhoun and Adams, "seeking political advantage," mixed up slavery and expansion; Wilmot introduced his "trouble-making Proviso as part of the political game"; the repeal clause in the Kansas-Nebraska Act was "the afterthought of a mere handful of politicians"; Chase's Appeal to the Independent Democrats was "false in its assertions and unfair in its purposes, but it was politically effective"; the "damaging" section in the Dred Scott decision was forced "by the political ambitions of dissenting judges." "These uncalled-for moves and this irresponsible leadership," concluded Craven, blew up a "crack-pot" crusade into national conflict.

It is hard to tell which was under attack here — the performance of a particular generation or democratic politics in general. But, if the indictment "blundering generation" meant no more than a general complaint that democratic politics placed a premium on emotionalism, then the Civil War would have been no more nor less "needless" than any event in our blundering history. The phrase "blundering generation" must consequently imply that the generation in power in the fifties was *below* the human or historical or democratic average in its blundering. Hence the third revisionist thesis:

(3) that the slavery problem could

have been solved without war. For, even if slavery were as unimportant as the revisionists have insisted, they would presumably admit that it constituted the real sticking-point in the relations between the sections. They must show therefore that there were policies with which a non-blundering generation could have resolved the slavery crisis and averted war; and that these policies were so obvious that the failure to adopt them indicated blundering and stupidity of a peculiarly irresponsible nature. If no such policies could be produced even by hindsight, then it would seem excessive to condemn the politicians of the fifties for failing to discover them at the time.

The revisionists have shown only a most vague and sporadic awareness of this problem. "Any kind of sane policy in Washington in 1860 might have saved the day for nationalism," remarked Craven; but he did not vouchsafe the details of these sane policies; we would be satisfied to know about one. Similarly Randall declared that there were few policies of the fifties he would wish repeated if the period were to be lived over again; but he was not communicative about the policies he would wish pursued. Nevins likewise blamed the war on the "collapse of American statesmanship," but restrained himself from suggesting how a non-collapsible statesmanship would have solved the hard problems of the fifties.

In view of this reticence on a point so crucial to the revisionist argument, it is necessary to reconstruct the possibilities that might lie in the back of revisionism. Clearly there could be only two "solutions" to the slavery problem: the preservation of slavery, or its abolition.

Presumably the revisionists would not regard the preservation of slavery as a possible solution. Craven, it is true, has argued that "most of the incentives to honest and sustained effort, to a contented, well-rounded life, might be found under slavery. . . . What owning and being owned added to the normal relationship of employer and employee is very hard to say." In describing incidents in which slaves beat up masters, he has even noted that "happenings and reactions like these were the rule [sic], not the exception." But Craven would doubtless admit that, however jolly this system might have been, its perpetuation would have been, to say the least, impracticable.

If, then, revisionism has rested on the assumption that the non-violent abolition of slavery was possible, such abolition could conceivably have come about through internal reform in the South; through economic exhaustion of the slavery system in the South; or through some government project for gradual and compensated emancipation. Let us examine these possibilities.

1. *The internal reform argument.* The South, the revisionists have suggested, might have ended the slavery system if left to its own devices; only the abolitionists spoiled everything by letting loose a hysteria which caused the southern ranks to close in self-defense.

This revisionist argument would have been more convincing if the decades of alleged anti-slavery feeling in the South had produced any concrete results. As one judicious southern historian, Professor Charles S. Sydnor, recently put it, "Although the abolition movement was followed by a decline of antislavery sentiment in the South, it must be remembered that in all the long years before that movement began no part of the South had made substantial progress toward ending slavery. . . . Southern liberalism had not ended slavery in any state."

In any case, it is difficult for historians seriously to suppose that northerners could have denied themselves feelings of disapproval over slavery. To say that there "should" have been no abolitionists in America before the Civil War is about as sensible as to say that there "should" have been no anti-Nazis in the nineteen-thirties or that there "should" be no anti-Communists today. People who indulge in criticism of remote evils may not be so pure of heart as they imagine; but that fact does not affect their inevitability as part of the historic situation.

Any theory, in short, which expects people to repress such spontaneous aversions is profoundly unhistorical. If revisionism has based itself on the conviction that things would have been different if only there had been no abolitionists, it has forgotten that abolitionism was as definite and irrevocable a factor in the historic situation as was slavery itself. And, just as abolitionism was inevitable, so too was the southern reaction against it — a reaction which, as Professor Clement Eaton has ably shown, steadily drove the free discussion of slavery out of the South. The extinction of free discussion meant, of course, the absolute extinction of any hope of abolition through internal reform.

2. *The economic exhaustion argument.* Slavery, it has been pointed out, was on the skids economically. It was overcapitalized and inefficient; it immobilized both capital and labor; its one-crop system was draining the soil of fertility; it stood in the way of industrialization. As the South came to realize these facts, a revisionist might argue, it would have moved to abolish slavery for its own economic good. As Craven put it, slavery "may have been almost ready to break down of its own weight."

This argument assumed, of course, that

southerners would have recognized the causes of their economic predicament and taken the appropriate measures. Yet such an assumption would be plainly contrary to history and to experience. From the beginning the South has always blamed its economic shortcomings, not on its own economic ruling class and its own inefficient use of resources, but on northern exploitation. Hard times in the eighteen-fifties produced in the South, not a reconsideration of the slavery system, but blasts against the North for the high prices of manufactured goods. The overcapitalization of slavery led, not to criticisms of the system, but to increasingly insistent demands for the reopening of the slave trade. Advanced southern writers like George Fitzhugh and James D. B. DeBow were even arguing that slavery was adapted to industrialism. When Hinton R. Helper did advance before the Civil War an early version of Craven's argument, asserting that emancipation was necessary to save the southern economy, the South burned his book. Nothing in the historical record suggests that the southern ruling class was preparing to deviate from its traditional pattern of self-exculpation long enough to take such a drastic step as the abolition of slavery.

3. *Compensated emancipation.* Abraham Lincoln made repeated proposals of compensated emancipation. In his annual message to Congress of December 1, 1862, he set forth a detailed plan by which States, on an agreement to abolish slavery by 1900, would receive government bonds in proportion to the number of slaves emancipated. Yet, even though Lincoln's proposals represented a solution of the problem conceivably gratifying to the slaveholder's purse as well as to his pride, they got nowhere. Two-thirds of the border representatives re-

jected the scheme, even when personally presented to them by Lincoln himself. And, of course, only the pressure of war brought compensated emancipation its limited hearing of 1862.

Still, granted these difficulties, does it not remain true that other countries abolished slavery without internal convulsion? If emotionalism had not aggravated the situation beyond hope, Craven has written, then slavery "might have been faced as a national question and dealt with as successfully as the South American countries dealt with the same problem." If Brazil could free its slaves and Russia its serfs in the middle of the nineteenth century without civil war, why could not the United States have done as well?

The analogies are appealing but not, I think, really persuasive. There are essential differences between the slavery question in the United States and the problems in Brazil or in Russia. In the first place, Brazil and Russia were able to face servitude "as a national question" because it was, in fact, a national question. Neither country had the American problem of the identification of compact sectional interests with the survival of the slavery system. In the second place, there was no race problem at all in Russia; and, though there was a race problem in Brazil, the more civilized folkways of that country relieved racial differences of the extreme tension which they breed in the South of the United States. In the third place, neither in Russia nor in Brazil did the abolition of servitude involve constitutional issues; and the existence of these issues played a great part in determining the form of the American struggle.

It is hard to draw much comfort, therefore, from the fact that other nations abolished servitude peaceably. The problem in America was peculiarly recalcitrant. The schemes for gradual emancipation got nowhere. Neither internal reform nor economic exhaustion contained much promise for a peaceful solution. The hard fact, indeed, is that the revisionists have not tried seriously to describe the policies by which the slavery problem could have been peacefully resolved. They have resorted instead to broad affirmations of faith: if only the conflict could have been staved off long enough, then somehow, somewhere, we could have worked something out. It is legitimate, I think, to ask how? where? what? — at least, if these affirmations of faith are to be used as the premise for castigating the unhappy men who had the practical responsibility for finding solutions and failed.

Where have the revisionists gone astray? In part, the popularity of revisionism obviously parallels that of *Gone with the Wind* — the victors paying for victory by pretending literary defeat. But the essential problem is why history should be so vulnerable to this literary fashion; and this problem, I believe, raises basic questions about the whole modern view of history. It is perhaps stating the issue in too portentous terms. Yet I cannot escape the feeling that the vogue of revisionism is connected with the modern tendency to seek in optimistic sentimentalism an escape from the severe demands of moral decision; that it is the offspring of our modern sentimentality which at once evades the essential problems in the name of a superficial objectivity and asserts their unimportance in the name of an invincible progress.

The revisionists first glided over the implications of the fact that the slavery system was producing a closed society in the South. Yet that society increasingly had justified itself by a political and philosophical repudiation of free society; southern thinkers swiftly developed the anti-libertarian potentialities in a social system whose cornerstone, in Alexander H. Stephens's proud phrase, was human bondage. In theory and practice, the South organized itself with mounting rigor against ideas of human dignity and freedom, because such ideas inevitably threatened the basis of their own system. Professor Frank L. Owsley, the southern agrarian, has described inadvertently but accurately the direction in which the slave South was moving. "The abolitionists and their political allies were threatening the existence of the South as seriously as the Nazis threaten the existence of England," wrote Owsley in 1940; ". . . Under such circumstances the surprising thing is that so little was done by the South to defend its existence."

There can be no question that many southerners in the fifties had similar sentiments; that they regarded their system of control as ridiculously inadequate; and that, with the book-burning, the censorship of the mails, the gradual illegalization of dissent, the South was in process of creating a real machinery of repression in order more effectively "to defend its existence." No society, I suppose, encourages criticism of its basic institutions. Yet, when a democratic society acts in self-defense, it does so at least in the name of human dignity and freedom. When a society based on bond slavery acts to eliminate criticism of its peculiar institution, it outlaws what a believer in democracy can only regard as the abiding values of man. When the basic institutions are evil, in other words, the effect of attempts to defend their existence can only be the moral and intellectual stultification of the society.

A society closed in the defense of evil institutions thus creates moral differences far too profound to be solved by compromise. Such a society forces upon every one, both those living at the time and those writing about it later, the necessity for a moral judgment; and the moral judgment in such cases becomes an indispensable factor in the historical understanding.

The revisionists were commendably anxious to avoid the vulgar errors of the post-Civil War historians who pronounced smug individual judgments on the persons involuntarily involved in the tragedy of the slave system. Consequently they tried hard to pronounce no moral judgments at all on slavery. Slavery became important, in Craven's phrase, "only as a very ancient labor system, probably at this time rather near the end of its existence"; the attempt to charge this labor system with moral meanings was "a creation of inflamed imaginations." Randall, talking of the Kansas-Nebraska Act, could describe it as "a law intended to subordinate the slavery question and hold it in *proper* proportion" (my italics). I have quoted Randall's even more astonishing argument that, because major controversies between downstate and metropolis in Illinois stopped short of war, there was reason to believe that the Civil War could have been avoided. Are we to take it that the revisionists seriously believe that the downstate-metropolis fight in Illinois — or the agrarian-industrial fight in the Coolidge and Hoover administrations — were in any useful sense comparable to the difference between the North and South in 1861?

Because the revisionists felt no moral urgency themselves, they deplored as fanatics those who did feel it, or brushed aside their feelings as the artificial product of emotion and propaganda. The revisionist hero was Stephen A. Douglas, who always thought that the great moral

problems could be solved by sleight-of-hand. The phrase "northern man of southern sentiments," Randall remarked, was "said opprobriously . . . as if it were a base thing for a northern man to work with his southern fellows."

By denying themselves insight into the moral dimension of the slavery crisis, in other words, the revisionists denied themselves a historical understanding of the intensities that caused the crisis. It was the moral issue of slavery, for example, that gave the struggles over slavery in the territories or over the enforcement of the fugitive slave laws their significance. These issues, as the revisionists have shown with cogency, were not in themselves basic. But they were the available issues; they were almost the only points within the existing constitutional framework where the moral conflict could be faced; as a consequence, they became charged with the moral and political dynamism of the central issue. To say that the Civil War was fought over the "unreal" issue of slavery in the territories is like saying that the Second World War was fought over the "unreal" issue of the invasion of Poland. The democracies could not challenge fascism inside Germany any more than opponents of slavery could challenge slavery inside the South; but the extension of slavery, like the extension of fascism, was an act of aggression which made a moral choice inescapable.

Let us be clear what the relationship of moral judgment to history is. Every historian, as we all know in an argument that surely does not have to be repeated in 1949, imports his own set of moral judgments into the writing of history by the very process of interpretation; and the phrase "every historian" includes the category "revisionist." Mr. De Voto in his paraphrases of the revisionist position has put admirably the contradictions on this point: as for "moral questions, God forbid. History will not put itself in the position of saying that any thesis may have been wrong, any cause evil. . . . History will not deal with moral values, though of course the Republican radicals were, well, culpable." The whole revisionist attitude toward abolitionists and radicals, repeatedly characterized by Randall as "unctuous" and "intolerant," overflows with the moral feeling which is so virtuously excluded from discussions of slavery.

An acceptance of the fact of moral responsibility does not license the historian to roam through the past ladling out individual praise and blame: such an attitude would ignore the fact that all individuals, including historians, are trapped in a web of circumstance which curtails their moral possibilities. But it does mean that there are certain essential issues on which it is necessary for the historian to have a position if he is to understand the great conflicts of history. These great conflicts are relatively few because there are few enough historical phenomena which we can confidently identify as evil. The essential issues appear, moreover, not in pure and absolute form, but incomplete and imperfect, compromised by the deep complexity of history. Their proponents may often be neurotics and fanatics, like the abolitionists. They may attain a social importance only when a configuration of non-moral factors — economic, political, social, military — permit them to do so.

Yet neither the nature of the context nor the pretensions of the proponents alter the character of the issue. And human slavery is certainly one of the few issues of whose evil we can be sure. It is not just "a very ancient labor system"; it is also a betrayal of the basic values

of our Christian and democratic tradition. No historian can understand the circumstances which led to its abolition until he writes about it in its fundamental moral context. "History is supposed to understand the difference between a decaying economy and an expanding one," as Mr. De Voto well said, "between solvency and bankruptcy, between a dying social idea and one coming to world acceptance. . . . It is even supposed to understand implications of the difference between a man who is legally a slave and one who is legally free."

"Revisionism in general has no position," De Voto continues, "but only a vague sentiment." Professor Randall well suggested the uncritical optimism of that sentiment when he remarked, "To suppose that the Union could not have been continued or slavery outmoded without the war and without the corrupt concomitants of war is hardly an enlightened assumption." We have here a touching afterglow of the admirable nineteenth-century faith in the full rationality and perfectibility of man; the faith that the errors of the world would all in time be "outmoded" (Professor Randall's use of this word is suggestive) by progress. Yet the experience of the twentieth century has made it clear that we gravely overrated man's capacity to solve the problems of existence within the terms of history.

This conclusion about man may disturb our complacencies about human nature. Yet it is certainly more in accord with history than Professor Randall's "enlightened" assumption that man can solve peaceably all the problems which overwhelm him. The unhappy fact is that man occasionally works himself into a log-jam; and that the log-jam must be burst by violence. We know that well enough from the experience of the last decade. Are we to suppose that some future historian will echo Professor Nevins' version of the "failure" of the eighteen-fifties and write: "The primary task of statesmanship in the nineteen-thirties was to furnish a workable adjustment between the United States and Germany, while offering strong inducements to the German people to abandon the police state and equal persuasions to the Americans to help the Nazis rather than scold them"? Will some future historian adapt Professor Randall's formula and write that the word "appeaser" was used "opprobriously" as if it were a "base" thing for an American to work with his Nazi fellow? Obviously this revisionism of the future (already foreshadowed in the work of Charles A. Beard) would represent, as we now see it, a fantastic evasion of the hard and unpleasant problems of the thirties. I doubt whether our present revisionism would make much more sense to the men of the eighteen-fifties.

The problem of the inevitability of the Civil War, of course, is in its essence a problem devoid of meaning. The revisionist attempt to argue that the war could have been avoided by "any kind of sane policy" is of interest less in its own right than as an expression of a characteristically sentimental conception of man and of history. And the great vogue of revisionism in the historical profession suggests, in my judgment, ominous weaknesses in the contemporary attitude toward history.

We delude ourselves when we think that history teaches us that evil will be "outmoded" by progress and that politics consequently does not impose on us the necessity for decision and for struggle. If historians are to understand the full-ness of the social dilemma they seek to reconstruct, they must understand that sometimes there is no escape from the implacabilities of moral decision. When social conflicts embody great moral issues, these conflicts cannot be assigned for solution to the invincible march of progress; nor can they be bypassed with "objective" neutrality. Not many problems perhaps force this decision upon the historian. But, if any problem does in our history, it is the Civil War.

To reject the moral actuality of the Civil War is to foreclose the possibility of an adequate account of its causes. More than that, it is to misconceive and grotesquely to sentimentalize the nature of history. For history is not a redeemer, promising to solve all human problems in time; nor is man capable of transcending the limitations of his being. Man generally is entangled in insoluble problems; history is consequently a tragedy in which we are all involved, whose keynote is anxiety and frustration, not progress and fulfillment. Nothing exists in history to assure us that the great moral dilemmas can be resolved without pain; we cannot therefore be relieved from the duty of moral judgment on issues so appalling and inescapable as those involved in human slavery; nor can we be consoled by sentimental theories about the needlessness of the Civil War into regarding our own struggles against evil as equally needless.

One must emphasize, however, that this duty of judgment applies to issues. Because we are all implicated in the same tragedy, we must judge the men of the past with the same forbearance and charity which we hope the future will apply toward us.

Suggestions for Additional Reading

The context in which Lincoln developed his policies is ably treated in Allan Nevins' general history of the Civil War period. Four volumes have thus far appeared: *Ordeal of the Union*, 2 vols. (New York, 1947) and *The Emergence of Lincoln*, 2 vols. (New York, 1950). Particular aspects of this context have been analyzed in detail in a great many studies. Among the more valuable are: Dwight L. Dumond, *Anti-Slavery Origins of the Civil War in the United States* (Ann Arbor, 1939) on the abolitionist movement; Avery O. Craven, *The Growth of Southern Nationalism, 1848–1861* (Baton Rouge, 1953) and Dwight L. Dumond, *The Secession Movement, 1860–1861* (New York, 1931) on the Southern movement for independence; Kenneth M. Stampp, *The Peculiar Institution* (New York, 1956) on the place of slavery in Southern life; Roy F. Nichols, *The Disruption of American Democracy* (New York, 1948) on the impact of the slavery question on the Democratic Party; and Reinhard H. Luthin, *The First Lincoln Campaign* (Cambridge, 1944) on the role of the slavery issue in the growth of the Republican Party.

Lincoln's views on the slavery question and their roots in his earlier life are described in Benjamin P. Thomas, *Abraham Lincoln* (New York, 1952). A more detailed account of Lincoln's pre-presidential years can be found in Albert J. Beveridge, *Abraham Lincoln, 1809–1858*, 2 vols. (Boston and New York, 1928) and a fuller discussion of the presidential years is presented in James G. Randall and Richard N. Current, *Lincoln the President*, 4 vols. (New York, 1946–1955). Among the studies which provide insights into individual facets of Lincoln's career, five are particularly valuable: James G. Randall, *Lincoln the Liberal Statesman* (New York, 1947); David Donald, *Lincoln Reconsidered* (New York, 1956); Stanley Pargellis, "Lincoln's Political Philosophy," *Abraham Lincoln Quarterly*, Vol. 3, (1945), pp. 275–290; T. Harry Williams, "Abraham Lincoln — Principle and Pragmatism in American Politics," *Mississippi Valley Historical Review*, Vol. 40, pp. 89–106; and Edmund Wilson, "Abraham Lincoln: The Union As Religious Mysticism," *Eight Essays* (New York, 1954). Carl Sandburg's multi-volume study, *Abraham Lincoln: The Prairie Years*, 2 vols. (New York, 1926) and *Abraham Lincoln: The War Years*, 4 vols. (New York, 1939) is valuable for its poetic insight into Lincoln's feelings. Lincoln's own writings and speeches should be read for an understanding of the literary and political style which was a vital aspect of Lincoln's character. Lincoln's debates with Douglas are reproduced in Paul M. Angle, ed., *Created Equal? The Complete Lincoln-Douglas Debates* (Chicago, 1958). The most complete collection of Lincoln's works is Roy P. Basler, ed., *The Collected Works of Abraham Lincoln*, 9 vols. (New Brunswick, 1953–1955).

Lincoln's role in the events immediately preceding the Civil War is treated in David M. Potter, *Lincoln and His Party in the Secession Crisis* (New Haven, 1942); Kenneth M. Stampp, *And the War Came* (Baton Rouge, 1950); and William E. Baringer, *A House Dividing: Lincoln as President Elect* (Springfield, 1945). The decision to send an expedition to Fort Sumter has been the subject of a controversy concerning Lincoln's intentions. Charles W. Ramsdell, "Lincoln and Fort Sumter," *Journal of Southern History*, III (August, 1937), pp. 259–288 argues that the expedition to Fort Sumter was deliberately designed to provoke the South into firing on Union troops, thus providing an excuse for beginning the war. James G. Randall, "When War Came in 1861," *Abraham Lincoln Quarterly*, I (March, 1940), pp. 3–42, and David M. Potter, *Lincoln and His Party in the Secession Crisis*, maintain that Lincoln's Sumter policy was designed to avoid war while preserving a semblance of Union authority in the South. Kenneth M. Stampp, "Lincoln and the Strategy of Defense in the Crisis of 1861," *Journal of Southern History*, XI (August, 1945), pp. 297–323, takes the position that Lincoln was primarily concerned neither with war nor with peace but rather was determined to maintain the Union through peaceful means if possible but through war if necessary.

The varied attitudes of Lincoln's contemporaries toward his policies are reflected in the editorial comments of Northern and Southern newspapers during the secession crisis. Representative editorials are reprinted in Howard C. Perkins, ed., *Northern Editorials on Secession*, 2 vols. (New York, 1942) and Dwight L. Dumond, ed., *Southern Editorials on Secession* (New York, 1931). A legalistic defense of the movement

toward secession by the Vice President of the Confederacy is Alexander H. Stephens, *A Constitutional View of the Late War Between the States*, 2 vols. (Philadelphia, 1868–1870).

Modern historians are divided in their attitudes toward the alternatives available to Lincoln in the secession crisis. George Fort Milton, *The Eve of Conflict: Stephen A. Douglas and the Needless War* (Boston and New York, 1934) is sympathetic to Douglas and his efforts to work out a compromise between North and South. Kenneth M. Stampp, *And The War Came* suggests that once the efforts toward compromise had failed, it would have been the better part of wisdom to let the Southern States "go in peace." Allan Nevins, *The Emergence of Lincoln* maintains that Lincoln followed the wisest course in opposing Southern secession with Northern power.

The evaluation of Lincoln's role in the events preceding the outbreak of war may depend largely upon an estimate of the moral validity of the war itself. Among modern historians, Avery Craven and James G. Randall are the outstanding proponents of the view that the Civil War was a national tragedy brought about by "a blundering generation" of politicians. Craven's views are developed in *The Repressible Conflict* (Baton Rouge, 1939), *The Coming of the Civil War* (New York, 1942), and "The Coming of the War Between the States: An Interpretation," *Journal of Southern History*, II (1936), pp. 303–322. Randall's position is set forth in *The Civil War and Reconstruction* (New York, 1937), "The Civil War Restudied," *Journal of Southern History*, VI (1940), pp. 439–457, and "The Blundering Generation," *Mississippi Valley Historical Review* XXVII (1940), pp. 3–28. The contrary view that the moral conflict over slavery provided sufficient justification for the policies of Northern leaders is presented by: Bernard De Voto, "The Easy Chair," *Harper's Magazine*, v. 192 (1946), pp. 123–126, 234–237; Arthur Schlesinger, Jr., review of *Ordeal of The Union* in *The Saturday Review of Literature*, XXX (October 18, 1947), pp. 9–10, and review of *The Emergence of Lincoln* in *The Christian Science Monitor* (October 14, 1953), p. 7; and Oscar Handlin, review of *The Emergence of Lincoln* in *The Nation*, v. 171 (1950), p. 513.

At the root of this debate is the fundamental question of the use of war as an instrument of national policy. This question has been a major concern of philosophers and political scientists down through the ages. In our own time, two leading advocates of alternative views on this question are Reinhold Niebuhr and Bertrand Russell. Niebuhr defends the use of force in *Moral Man and Immoral Society* (New York, 1932) on the grounds that justice in social relations cannot be secured solely by appeals to reason. Russell argues against the resort to force in "Philosophy and Politics," *Unpopular Essays* (New York, 1950) and *Why Men Fight* (New York, 1916) on the grounds that the results of war are in almost all cases less desirable from an ethical standpoint than the consequences of peaceful alternatives.